A New Hope

ACA
Beginner's
Handbook

ACA SERENITY PRAYER / STATEMENT

Higher Power/God/Spirit/Universe/Life/etc.
Grant(s) me the serenity
to accept the people
I cannot change
the courage to change
the one I can
and the wisdom to know
that one is me

A New Hope

ACA
Beginner's
Handbook

**Adult Children of Alcoholics®/
Dysfunctional Families**

Copyright © 2024 by

Adult Children of Alcoholics®
World Service Organization, Inc.
Post Office Box 811
Lakewood, California USA 90714
www.adultchildren.org

All rights reserved. No part of this publication may be reproduced, stored in a retrieval system or transmitted in any form or by any means, electronic, mechanical, photocopying, recording, or otherwise, without the written permission of the publisher.

Author: Adult Children of Alcoholics®/Dysfunctional Families

Title: A New Hope

ISBN 978-1-944840-62-4

1st Edition, 1st Printing, 2024
Printed in the UK

1 2 3 4 5   28 27 26 25 24

Table of contents

Introduction — 6

Handbook chapters
Chapter 1: Welcome to ACA — 8
Chapter 2: ACA Problem (Laundry Lists Traits) — 10
Chapter 3: Family Dysfunction — 12
Chapter 4: ACA Solution — 16
Chapter 5: True Self / False Self — 20
Chapter 6: Inner Critical Parent — 22
Chapter 7: Inner Loving Parent — 24
   Supplement—Inner Loving Parent — 26
Chapter 8: Inner Child — 28
   Supplement—ACA Reparenting Techniques — 30
Chapter 9: Twelve Steps in ACA — 32
Chapter 10: Step 1 Introduction — 34
Chapter 11: Spirituality — 36
Chapter 12: Childhood Trauma — 38
Chapter 13: Grief — 40
Chapter 14: Relationships — 42
Chapter 15: Fellow Travelers — 44
   Supplement—ACA Fellow Traveler and Resources — 46
Chapter 16: Service — 48
Chapter 17: ACA Promises — 50

Appendices — 55
Appendix A: Sample ACA Beginner's Meeting Format — 56
Appendix B: Sharing in ACA Meetings, Cross Talk & Fixing — 60
Appendix C: ACA 12 Step Workgroups Resources — 62
Appendix D: Handbook Purpose & Stated Perspectives — 66
Appendix E: ACA Foundational Materials — 68
   Laundry List Traits (assessment) — 70
   Other / Opposite Laundry List (assessment) — 71
   The Complete Laundry List Framework — 72
   The ACA Problem — 74
   The ACA Solution — 75
   ACA 12 Steps — 76
   Tony A.'s Version of the 12 Steps — 77
   ACA 12 Traditions — 78
   The ACA Promises — 79

INTRODUCTION

The ACA fellowship text, the Big Red Book, is a life-saving resource, but it can be daunting and overwhelming for program beginners. And for some newcomers, the idea of immediately diving into ACA 12 Step work can be terrifying.

We who developed this Handbook decided in late 2018 to start a local meeting specifically for ACA beginners. We developed introductory materials to support and guide those attending that meeting. While there is no single path to healing the effects of childhood trauma through ACA, our goal was to create a clear, concise, comprehensive ACA Beginner's Handbook that includes:

- Topic summaries: 1) written specifically for beginners to address fundamental concepts in ACA recovery, 2) derived from existing ACA literature, and 3) that can be read and discussed manageably within a one-hour meeting timeframe.
- Questions on each topic that participants can: 1) draw from to help frame their initial personal shares at meetings, 2) use as a tool to connect with other participants outside of the meetings, and 3) experience as preparation for more in-depth program work.
- References pointing to optional further reading on each topic in existing ACA literature (texts, workbooks, tri-folds, booklets, etc.).
- Fundamental program materials (the Problem / Laundry Lists Traits, the ACA Solution, the 12 Steps, the 12 Traditions & the ACA Promises) as well as other supplemental resources, tools, and exercises.

A New Hope ACA Beginner's Handbook slowly brings program participants out of isolation through a predictable, structured format so they are less likely to feel overwhelmed. More intensive reparenting practices and Step work can begin when participants determine they are ready. Originally designed as a beginner's meeting format, this Handbook is also commonly used one-on-one between program members and as part of small workgroups. Additional notes on the rationale for Handbook content selection, presentation order, program perspectives, and style choices can be found in Appendix D, "About this Handbook."

We, the authors, are grateful for the immeasurable support we received during the development of this Handbook. Now that A New Hope has been accepted for publication by the ACA Literature Committee and World Services Organization (WSO), we look forward to receiving additional feedback during the full fellowship review process. Please share your comments and ideas at: https://acawso.org/feedback-on-existing-literature

NOTES

Chapter 1
WELCOME TO ACA

The purpose of ACA is threefold—to shelter and support newcomers in confronting denial; to comfort those mourning their early loss of security, trust, and love; and to teach the skills for reparenting ourselves with gentleness, humor, love, and respect.

In childhood, our identity is shaped through attachments—the reflections of ourselves we see in the eyes of our caregivers. As small children, we fear losing this reflection—thinking the mirror defines us and makes us real, and that we disappear or have no self without it. However, the distorted self-image many adult children developed through family dysfunction is not who we are. Nor are we the wounded child still hiding all alone behind our false masks.

Moving from isolation is the first step an adult child makes in recovering the self. Isolation can be both a prison and a sanctuary. Adult children, suspended between need and fear—frozen between fight or flight—agonize in the middle and resolve the tension by explosive bursts of rebellion, or silently enduring the despair. Isolation is our retreat from the paralyzing pain of indecision. The simple act of showing up at an ACA meeting opens the door to healing and freedom.

The return of feelings, often a painful part of the mourning process, indicates healing has begun. Initial feelings of anger, guilt, rage, and despair resolve into a final acceptance of loss. Genuine grieving for our childhood ends our morbid fascination with the past. It lets us return to the present, free to live fully as adults. Sharing the burden of grief other adult children feel gives us the courage and strength to face our own grief. The pain of mourning and grief is eventually balanced with the freedom to fully love and care for someone and experience joy in life.

Through ACA reparenting, we give ourselves the love we need by releasing our shame and blame, and embracing the child inside. With a child's sensitivity, we reach out to explore the world again and become aware of the need to trust and love others. With help from our ACA fellow travelers, we gently discover how to fill in the nurturing and attention we did not receive as children. We learn to become our own loving parent. In time, the aspects of ourselves we thought we had lost become valuable parts of our new inner compass.

In ACA, we stop believing we have no worth. We start to see our true identity, reflected in the eyes of other adult children, as the strong survivors and valuable people we actually are.

Chapter 1
QUESTIONS

1. What motivated me to explore ACA at this point in my life?

2. ACA describes the rules of family dysfunction as Don't talk—Don't trust—Don't feel. How did those rules apply in my childhood?

3. How do I usually feel about asking other people for help? What were my experiences in childhood if I asked for support from the adults in my life?

4. How have I physically isolated in my life? How have I emotionally isolated?

5. What do I hope the ACA program will bring me?

CHAPTER 1 OPTIONAL FURTHER READING

ACA Big Red Book
- "Introduction" – by Claudia B
- Chapter 2 – "It Will Never Happen to Me"
- Chapter 6 – "ACA – How It Works"

ACA Strengthening My Recovery (Daily Affirmations)
- January 18, p.19 – "A New Way of Life"
- June 18, p.176 – "Newcomers"
- August 23, p.244 – "Grief as Freedom"
- December 17, p.364 – "Expressing Feelings"

Chapter 2
ACA PROBLEM—LAUNDRY LISTS TRAITS

In ACA, we believe the experiences of growing up in a dysfunctional family affect us as adults. In just 260 words, The Laundry List describes the thinking and personality of an adult reared in dysfunction. When read aloud at an ACA meeting, The Laundry List (also written as "The Problem") can produce a sense of curiosity and identification that intuitively resonates with an adult child. The Laundry List represents expressions of childhood trauma commonly shared across our diverse membership.

These 14 Traits describe a personality who has difficulty loving another person, and accepting love, as well. This statement isn't meant to be shaming or intended to highlight hopelessness. As children and teens, we were not given consistent, healthy examples of love—so how can we know love or recognize it as adults? Our caregivers shamed, belittled, manipulated, or withheld their love and attention from us when we were vulnerable children. In their confusion, they may have called it love. They passed on what was done to them. What many adult children described as love or intimacy before reaching ACA was likely codependence or rigid control.

There is also a second list of adult child characteristics in ACA called the "Other" or "Opposite" Laundry List Traits. While the original Laundry List describes how we were directly wounded by family dysfunction in childhood, the Other Laundry List represents how we may have also learned to protect ourselves by becoming aggressors. In other words, by adopting our parents' behaviors, we "become" our parents. For example, if we feared authority figures as the first Laundry List Trait suggests, we may also have become authority figures to be feared by our children, spouse, co-workers, or others. Each of the Laundry Lists Traits, therefore, has an opposite Other Laundry List Trait ... just as damaging as their counterparts.

While all these Traits might be troublesome in our adult lives, they protected us as children. They were the flight, fight, or fawn mechanisms that allowed us to survive dangerous situations in our early years. Thus, we don't easily surrender our Traits even though they create the internal pain and isolation that has driven us to ACA. And whether we are expressing victim roles, behaving aggressively towards others, or reflexively fawning for approval in our adult lives, ACA recovery can help. The program isn't fast or easy. But the effort it takes to work ACA produces much healthier results than the effort it takes to maintain disconnected and dysfunctional lives. We will see amazing results if we shift some of the energy we expend on living in the Traits, instead, towards releasing them in our ACA work.

Chapter 2
QUESTIONS

1. With which of the Laundry List Traits (p.68) do I most and least identify?

2. With which of the Other Laundry List Traits (p.69) do I most and least identify?

3. Which of the Laundry List Traits or Other Laundry List Traits can I most easily trace back to ways I adapted to protect myself in childhood?

4. "Our Laundry Lists Traits are a legitimate reaction to long-term trauma." (Strengthening My Recovery, p.193). How do I feel about this statement?

5. What feelings come up for me when reading or hearing these Traits? What feelings arise when I think about softening, releasing, or healing them?

CHAPTER 2 OPTIONAL FURTHER READING

ACA Big Red Book
- "Welcome to ACA" – (pp. xii–xv)
- Chapter 1 – "The Laundry List—Problem" (p.3)

ACA Strengthening My Recovery (Daily Affirmations)
- January 12, p.13 – "Trait 1"
- June 28, p.186 – "Caretaking"
- July 4, p.193 – "Long-Term Trauma"
- December 24, p.371 – "The Problem"

Chapter 3
FAMILY DYSFUNCTION

Dysfunctional homes often, but not always, include alcoholism or other forms of addiction. Family dysfunction can occur in rigidly religious, militaristic, or punitive homes—or homes dominated by control, harsh judgment, and perfectionism. Any type of abuse or neglect creates dysfunctional home environments, as can parental mental illness or other forms of parental disability. Persistent debt or gambling can also be signs of family dysfunction, as can issues with food such as eating or dieting obsessions.

Did dysfunction exist in my childhood environment? This is something we each must decide for ourselves. Skeptics might say: "My parents could be harsh, but they meant well. I know they loved me and cared about me. They did the best they could." Is it possible these statements could be true, and the home was still dysfunctional?

Some adult children have few memories of childhood at all. Other adult children see no evidence of problems in their upbringing because the dysfunction seems normal or tolerable to them. Many adult children can recount the horrors of their childhood upbringing in great detail yet do so without feeling or without connecting to the deep sense of loss each event triggered.

Shame and abandonment are two of the most identifiable indications of a dysfunctional home. Among other factors, they are two of the conditions that help produce an adult child, whether alcohol or drugs are in the home or not. Adult children from all dysfunctional family types not only feel shame deeply, but often believe they are inherently shameful.

Perhaps evidence of being raised in a dysfunctional home might be seen initially in how people live their adult lives. Those who care for themselves cannot always point to a childhood event that let them know their parents valued them. However, their actions in adulthood demonstrate they care about themselves. Conversely, adult children cannot always point to an incident in their upbringing that let them know their parents didn't value them in the ways they needed. Yet what does it say when adults live forever caught in the Laundry List and Other Laundry List Traits, or lost in their addictions and other self-harming behaviors?

We are looking for the truth so that we can live our lives with choice and self-confidence. We want to break the cycle of family dysfunction. In ACA, we offer our parents fairness as we examine the family system with honesty.

Chapter 3
QUESTIONS

1. What types of dysfunction can I identify in my family of origin (see "Family Labels," next page)?

2. What memories do I have of fearing my parents or caregivers? What did I do with those fears as a child?

3. In what ways did I monitor my parents' or caregivers' feelings, moods, or behaviors in my childhood so I could do certain things to feel safer?

4. What connections am I starting to see between family dysfunction and how I have expressed the Laundry List and Other Laundry List Traits in my adult life?

5. In what ways are the relationships between family dysfunction, shame, and abandonment becoming more apparent to me?

CHAPTER 3 OPTIONAL FURTHER READING
ACA Big Red Book
- Chapter 2 – "It Will Never Happen to Me" (p.21)
- Chapter 3 – "My Parents Did Not Drink, But I Can Relate" (p.53)

ACA Strengthening My Recovery (Daily Affirmations)
- February 18, p.51 – "Abandonment"
- May 26, p.152 – "Fear"
- June 12, p.170 – "Shame"
- September 4, p.257 – "Generational Grief"

Chapter 3
FAMILY DYSFUNCTION SUPPLEMENT

Exploring Dysfunction in My History: Family Labels

This checklist is adapted from "Family Diagram Labels" (Big Red Book pp. 127 & 128). Below, think about your experiences or what you have heard about your family. Place a check next to each behavior/label that applies to one or more of your family members. While this list is not exhaustive, it can help to identify possible family dysfunction.

- **alcoholic** – heavy alcohol use/abuse ☐
- **drug addict** – heavy illicit substances use/abuse ☐
- **pill popper** – heavy prescriptions drug use/abuse ☐
- **emotionally ill/mental health issues** ☐
- **chronically ill physically** ☐
- **criminal behavior, incarceration** ☐
- **gambler** – looking for "big money wins" ☐
- **heavy debt** – always borrowing money or needless spending (likes showy "nice things") ☐
- **vanity** – always had a face in the mirror, intensely focused on outward appearance ☐
- **scarcity mentality** – never enough, don't throw out anything; possibly hoarding ☐
- **eating issues** – obesity; Bulimia or Anorexia; cyclical dieting ☐
- **food pusher** – great cook, food as an expression of "caring" or "reward" ☐
- **sexually aggressive** (overtly not safe) – grabbing, touching, pinching, wrestling, etc. ☐
- **sexually suggestive** (covertly not safe) – inappropriate language, exhibitionism, sexually "creepy" ☐
- **violent** – slapped, pushed, hit; glorified fighting ☐
- **passive-aggressive**; **controlling** – manipulation, false kindness, indirect aggression ☐
- **verbally abusive** – harsh, critical, judgmental, threatening, demeaning ☐
- **argumentative** – will not be quiet, keeps arguments going, all-or-nothing thinking ☐
- **workaholic** – worked a lot; views work as the measure of one's worth ☐
- **undependable** – does not follow through; promises not kept, lies ☐
- **religiously rigid** – judgmental, harsh, critical, controlling, all-or-nothing thinking ☐
- **militaristic** – punitive, harsh, rigid, perfectionistic, critical, controlling ☐
- **racist** – prejudice and antagonism towards other races; belief that one's race is superior to others ☐
- **sexist** – prejudice and antagonism around gender; belief one gender is superior to another ☐
- **homophobic** – prejudice towards gay men, lesbians, bisexual, and trans (LGBTQ+) people ☐
- **worrier/neurotic** – what can go wrong will go wrong, "the sky is falling" ☐
- **rescuer/co-dependent** – caught up in people's drama and chaos; focused on "helping" others ☐
- **enabler** – shields others from the natural consequences of their behavior; "caretaker" ☐
- **martyr** – suffers "for the benefit of others" and then wants recognition for their "sacrifices" ☐
- **hero family role** – "think positive," go big or go home, focused on outward appearances ☐
- **mascot family role** – constant joking; humor that can be harmful; can't deal with serious matters ☐
- **lost child family role** – loner, isolated, avoids conflict and confrontation ☐
- **scapegoat family role** – outcast; seen to cause family shame and embarrassment; rule-breaker ☐

Chapter 3
MY FAMILY MEMBERS

ACA 12 Step work (specifically, Step 1 in the Big Red Book or yellow ACA 12 Steps workbook) involves creating a comprehensive family diagram, including relatives on all sides of the family—parents, stepparents, other caregivers, siblings, grandparents, aunts, uncles, cousins, nieces, nephews, your own children, etc. Feel free to write down names of family members below, such as "mom," "Grandparent Kai," younger sibling "Adrian," etc. You can then explore how the Family Labels on the preceding page might apply to them and their behaviors. What, if anything, do you notice?

Chapter 4
ACA SOLUTION

"The ACA Solution is to become your own Loving Parent."

The process of ACA recovery requires us to become our own loving parent, relieving from duty our most ardent defender, our inner critical parent. Only then will our inner child begin to feel and express all the hurt inside. As we grow comfortable with the uncomfortable absence of our inner critical parent, we build trust that our loving parent will help our inner children feel safe and nurtured. Our internal intimacy translates into outward intimacy, and we are made whole once again.
—*"Strengthening My Recovery"* – p.110

Many adult children can be resistant to the notion of an inner loving parent that is thoughtful and affirming. They can more easily identify with an inner critical parent who is harsh or produces constant self-doubt from within. Many of us can accept that we have an inner critical parent, but resist the idea of a loving one.

Reparenting lovingly is not as foreign as it might sound. Most of us were forced to "play parent" to ourselves as children because our parents or relatives were not available in the ways we needed. In some homes, we met our own needs by preparing our own meals or washing our own clothes. In some cases, we tended to a sibling with more care than our dysfunctional caregivers. Some of us were provided with all our basic physical needs, and were perhaps even told we were loved. However, our parents were adult children themselves—out of touch with their feelings and incapable of true intimacy with us. And if we were aggressive or self-destructive as children, we can still see moments when we hoped for or believed in affectionate care and tenderness. We were all born with a part of us who knows the need to feel nurtured, protected, and valued. This is why the ACA healing path involves the inner child—a gateway to compassion and our new inner compass.

Learning to survive as children, however, and reparenting ourselves as adults have important distinctions. We were alone as children, or felt scared and lonely. We were forced to grow up too soon. But we are NOT alone today. Today, we have resources available to us that we didn't have as children, even if beyond our current awareness or understanding. Reparenting in ACA means giving ourselves the love we seek—the love we needed but didn't consistently receive as children. With some patience, a little courage, and support from our fellow travelers, we can learn to use the ACA recovery tools and reparenting techniques to gently heal the past. We discover how to connect with ourselves and others in safe and healthy ways.

Chapter 4
QUESTIONS

1. Like others coming into ACA, do I have resistance to the idea of reparenting? How do I feel about other similar terms like "self-nurturing" and "self-care?"

2. Who are some adults, real or imagined, that are good examples of loving parents? What do loving parents do to create safety and nurturing for children?

3. The ACA Solution (p.75) reads, "Our actual parent is a Higher Power whom some of us choose to call God." How do I feel about this statement, and what does it mean to me?

4. What parts of the ACA Solution (p.75) encourage us to break the old rules of family dysfunction: Don't talk, don't trust, and don't feel?

5. Which ACA recovery tools (see next page) most resonate with me, and which ones am I apprehensive about using? Which tools have I used in my life already?

CHAPTER 4 OPTIONAL FURTHER READING
ACA Big Red Book
- Chapter 8 – "The Solution: Becoming Your Own Loving Parent" (p.295)

Trifold Brochures
- ACA Is, section; "Tools of ACA Recovery" & "ACA Tool Bag"

ACA Strengthening My Recovery (Daily Affirmations)
- June 6, p.164 – "Beyond Survival"
- December 27, p.374 – "Grief and Tools"

The Loving Parent Guidebook
- Chapter 1 – "Introduction to Reparenting the Inner Family" (p.8)

Chapter 4
ACA SOLUTION SUPPLEMENT

ACA Tools of Recovery*

The ACA Solution is to "become your own loving parent." We learn to "reparent ourselves with gentleness, humor, love, and respect." Below are some of the suggested tools of ACA recovery that can help us in the reparenting process. We must recognize there are many recovery tools at our disposal. Each of us must decide which tools work well for us and how to best use them for our recovery.

- We go to ACA meetings.
- We read ACA literature.
- We risk moving out of isolation by reaching out and connecting directly with other fellow travelers.
- We start breaking the rules of family dysfunction: We begin to talk, trust, and feel. We begin to remember.
- We learn to sit quietly for short times (some call this prayer or meditation)
- We better understand all our needs, including our physical, emotional, psychological, intellectual, and spiritual needs.
- We practice communicating and upholding our boundaries.
- We create deeper, trusted connections with some fellow travelers (sponsors/co-sponsors/recovery partners) and build support networks.
- We use the ACA reparenting techniques (p. 30)** to:
  - Identify and learn to address our inner critical parent.
  - Recognize and strengthen our inner loving parent.
  - Connect with, nurture, protect and guide our inner child (children).
- We identify the people, places, and things that are healthy and useful to our lives today and release those that are not.
- We start formally working the ACA 12 Steps when ready.
- We give service in ACA, starting by showing up and being present for ourselves.

* Curated from across the BRB, ACA Is trifold & ACA Toolbag trifold
** ACA reparenting techniques addressed in BRB Chapter 8, pages 304–306. Please refer to ACA's Loving Parent Guidebook for comprehensive program reparenting resources.

Chapter 4
LIST OF MY PERSONAL RECOVERY TOOLS

Chapter 5
TRUE SELF/FALSE SELF

In ACA, some members refer to aspects of the child within as the true self—the original person, being, or energy we truly are. Some describe the true self as a divine inner spark, connecting us to powers greater than ourselves, and present during our spiritual awakenings. Some understand their adult true self as an inner healer—an anchor in the reparenting process. Some in ACA believe that childhood wounding forced us to hide our truth, and to develop a false self that could protect us from further harm … but at a devastating cost.

In our abusive and neglectful childhoods, we internalized our caregivers' wounds. We took responsibility for their dysfunction—believing we could make them love us if we played the right roles and wore the right masks. We felt something was wrong with us even though we couldn't put a finger on it. We believed we were shameful and perhaps even deserved to be abandoned. We may have even acted out shamefully or destructively to fulfill the false projections. As part of the abusive cycle, we began to repeat these lies to ourselves, and the internalization became complete: We accepted our false self as truth.

The false self in ACA is described as the adult child personality expressed through the Laundry Lists Traits. Many also see the false self as the family roles we instinctively adopted in childhood: hero, scapegoat, lost child, and mascot. The false self has been described as our addicted self, our codependent self, and our dissociated self. Some see the false self as an expression of their inner critical parent—control, all-or-nothing thinking, perfectionism, and harsh judgment. The false self was born out of protective childhood survival mechanisms that we carried into our adult lives. It is deeply anchored because it helped keep us alive as children under painful circumstances. In childhood, these masks and roles were sometimes the difference between life and death.

By living in our false self throughout our lives, we may have thought we had buried our true self permanently—but it has been there all along. The preciousness of the inner child was always tapping from within, asking and hoping for our truth to be acknowledged and embraced. In ACA recovery, many of us come to respect our false self for figuring out how to survive our childhood wounding. Through ACA reparenting, we release false self-expressions that no longer serve us, and learn to nurture, protect, and guide the authenticity we wish to reclaim. We find true self-compassion, true self-forgiveness, true self-esteem, and true self-love.

Chapter 5
QUESTIONS

1. What aspects or parts of me feel "true?" What parts of me feel "false?"

2. Complete this sentence: "I'm afraid if people knew the REAL me, they would …?"

3. What false self childhood role(s) did I adopt growing up in my dysfunctional home, such as hero, scapegoat (outcast), mascot (clown), and lost child? How did these roles seem to protect me?

4. What is the difference between false self-esteem and true self-esteem?

5. What are next steps I can take in my life today towards living in greater truth?

CHAPTER 5 OPTIONAL FURTHER READING:
ACA Big Red Book
- Chapter 1: "The Laundry List – Problem" (p.3)
- Chapter 7: "Part 1," section; "Making a Beginning" – family roles (pp.96–102)
- Chapter 8: "The Solution: Becoming Your Own Loving Parent" (p.295)
- Chapter 15: section; "Self-Love" (pp.434–442)

ACA Strengthening My Recovery (Daily Affirmations)
- January 4, p.5 – "False Self"
- February 15, p.48 – "Promise Two"
- February 17, p.50 – "Family Roles"
- May 8, p.134 – "Inner Child / True Self"

Chapter 6
INNER CRITICAL PARENT

Adult children arrive at ACA with hypercritical messages in their minds. We tend to judge ourselves or others without mercy. But where did these messages come from? Through the first 18 years of our lives, our families had 6,570 days to shame, belittle, ignore, withhold from, or manipulate us during the most formative years of our being. That's up to 160,000 hours of living with unhealthy parenting—72 seasons of sorrow stored deeply in the tissue of our bodies. This dysfunction was encoded into us as the false self, and it's maintained and reinforced in our adult lives by an inner critical parent.

The inner critical parent is a childhood part of us that arose and strengthened in the absence of unconditional love. It is the inner voice, images, feelings, or sensations that tell us we are not good enough, smart enough, or worthy enough ... that we are inherently and fundamentally broken, and that no one understands us. This inner critic repeats the harsh, aggressive messages from childhood that always find fault in actions, thoughts, and feelings—both in ourselves and in others. The critic is the internal sense of doubt, blame, or disgust that undermines our relationships and chances of authentic connection. The critical voice produces guilt feelings when we think about asking for what we need. Living with this inner critical parent can result in dissociation, depression, anxiety, panic, and if left unhealed, even death.

Many of us enter ACA feeling the effects of the inner critic but not knowing why. We may not become fully aware of this critic until we slow down enough to recognize it. We have become so comfortable with shaming, doubting, or cursing ourselves or others that we don't even notice the extreme harshness. Some say the inner critic can remain masked because it speaks to us in our own voice. Perfectionism, control, all-or-nothing thinking, and constant judgment are the distorted forms of thinking that power the inner critical parent.

As part of the ACA healing process, we learn to pay attention to our attitudes about ourselves and others, noting the harsh thoughts, doubts, and fears as they arise. Reparenting ourselves is based on our willingness to set boundaries with our inner critic and strengthen an inner loving parent who can connect with and care for the wounded child within. We learn to set limits and say "no" or "not now" to the critical parent, or ask it to step back or turn down the volume. We also work with the inner critic through Step work, for example, addressing the "powerlessness" we feel over the critic in Step 1. Using affirmations, journaling, and other techniques, we create some "breathing room," and learn to give ourselves and others a break.

Chapter 6
QUESTIONS

1. What messages did my parents or other adults in my childhood use to criticize, control, bully, ignore, scold, or shame me? How did I feel when this happened?

2. How might neglect or manipulative withholding of attention from childhood caregivers have contributed to the development of my inner critical parent?

3. Have I ever felt "crazy" but kept my feelings inside and never talked about these thoughts? If so, how might this relate to an inner critical parent?

4. In what ways does my inner critic express itself both inwardly and outwardly?

5. What are ways I can begin to recognize and set internal limits or boundaries with my inner critical parent when it arises?

CHAPTER 6 OPTIONAL FURTHER READING:
ACA Big Red Book
- Chapter 2: section; "Internalized Modes of Thinking and Acting" (pp.35–50)
- Chapter 8: section; "Identifying Our Inner Critical Parent" (pp.306–309)

ACA Strengthening My Recovery (Daily Affirmations)
- February 29, p.62 – "Guilt"
- April 4, p.99 – "Critical Parent"
- October 6, p.290 – "Inner Critic"

The Loving Parent Guidebook
- Chapter 5: "Identifying the Critical Parent" (p.46)

Chapter 7
INNER LOVING PARENT

Becoming our own loving parent is the ACA Solution, yet at first, this task may feel awkward or daunting. In many ways, reparenting is simple but not easy—and it's understandable to feel reluctance. Unfortunately, we can't go back in time and make our parents give us the unconditional love we didn't get. And no one else can replace that missing love today. So, with gentleness, humor, love, and respect, we discover how to connect inward with the most vulnerable parts of ourselves and compassionately reparent them. We learn to listen for and to feel our inner child.

When we connect to our child within, we can provide the nurturing, safety, and guidance most of us lacked as children. The inner child will usually not emerge, however, until we establish our inner loving parent—so we must first identify and encourage this loving presence inside. We can write a letter and use affirmations to awaken the calm, compassionate, curious, connected, and caring part of ourselves. We each have this type of love inside, regardless of what we might say or believe. Love is there, it is original, and through ACA, we learn to awaken it.

We further awaken the loving parent by listening to our inner self-talk and recognizing when it is harsh. The loving parent's role is to set boundaries with our critical, inner voice, and to care for, nurture, and protect the child within. We learn to stop mid-sentence if we put ourselves down or criticize our thoughts, feelings, or behaviors. We reframe our stumbles as opportunities to learn or grow emotionally. Setting healthy limits with the inner critic in this way is an act of love.

We will struggle, have doubts, and become frustrated in our recovery at times. We can do everything right and still wonder if we are making progress. An inner loving parent reminds us we are good enough and we are making progress … that our childhood wounding was not our fault and that we are OK. A loving parent provides unconditional love—the spiritual healing force and inoculation from shame that was missing in our childhoods, and which we use to reparent ourselves today. The loving parent creates a safe space to heal, sometimes drawing as needed from resources beyond our current understanding.

With effort, patience, and support from our ACA fellow travelers, our inner loving parent awakens. We grow more comfortable with our new, healthier self-talk. We choose to believe the affirming messages from our loving parent over our critical parent's harsh messages. We can feel more at peace as we better understand our feelings, wants, and needs. As we strengthen our inner loving parent, emotional safety opens for our child within, and new depths of healing can begin.

Chapter 7
QUESTIONS

1. How would I envision a loving adult caring for an abused or neglected child? How might I see myself caring for a small child in emotional pain?

2. In what ways did I take care of myself (or siblings) as a child that my inner loving parent can draw upon for my own self-care today?

3. When is a time in my life I can recall feeling a tender, internal loving presence?

4. Remembering a painful time in my childhood when I felt alone … what could a caring, compassionate, unconditionally loving adult presence have said or done to help me know I was safe and mattered (see affirmations, next page)?

5. In what ways does an inner loving parent fit or not fit into my spiritual beliefs? How do I understand my loving parent in relation to higher or greater power?

CHAPTER 7 OPTIONAL FURTHER READING:
ACA Big Red Book
- Chapter 8: section; "Loving Parent" (pp.298–302)
- Chapter 8: section; "What is a Loving Parent" testimonials (pp.309–310)

ACA Strengthening My Recovery (Daily Affirmations)
- May 12, p.138 – "Responding with Love"
- July 5, p.194 – "Inner Loving Parent"
- August 7, p.228 – "Unconditional Love"

The Loving Parent Guidebook
- Chapter 2: "Awakening Your Loving Parent" (p.21)

Chapter 7
INNER LOVING PARENT SUPPLEMENT

Loving Parent Letter
(adapted from BRB p.299)

ACA suggests several ways to help awaken our internal love. One technique is writing a letter:

> *"Dear Inner Loving Parent (or caring part of myself),*
> *Please allow me to be gentler and more accepting of myself. Please help me to stop judging myself so harshly. Please let me focus on progress rather than perfection..."*

We can keep this letter handy and read it regularly, adding to it as we wish. Of course, writing a letter like this won't change everything right away. Still, it can demonstrate to our inner child that we are willing to find new ways to set boundaries with our inner critic. This simple letter can signify a powerful shift, moving away from self-abandonment and towards self-love, self-nurturing, and self-compassion ... towards healthy reparenting.

Reparenting Affirmations
(complete listing on BRB pp. 329–330)

Affirmations can be thought of as a language that develops between an inner loving parent and the child within. In time, this language replaces the voice of the harsh inner critical parent. Many of the ACA reparenting affirmations begin with:

"It's OK"

It's OK ... to trust, to cry, to hope, to make a mistake, to say I don't know, to say "no," etc. There are no specific words or phrases that work for everyone as affirmations—we must each find our own loving inner language that feels right. "It's OK" can be a great place to start.

The reparenting process requires some experimentation at first, and can feel strange. It can seem awkward to break the old rules of family dysfunction: Don't Talk—Don't trust—Don't feel. Some adult children resist this exercise because they find the words they are saying difficult to believe ... and that's OK. Simple, heartfelt affirmations have helped many adult children neutralize the inner critic and learn to trust that their childhood wounding was not their fault. As the critic's power recedes, and the loving parent awakens and strengthens, we find healing for our child within.

Chapter 7
REPARENTING AFFIRMATIONS THAT WORK WELL FOR ME

Chapter 8
INNER CHILD

For many ACA members, the child within is our original being; the innocent part of us that existed before we were shattered and broken. Our inner child has original trust, original belief, and original love. Our child within understands feelings and can help connect us to powers greater than ourselves. Becoming our own loving parent—reparenting ourselves—is the gateway to our child within.

Family dysfunction drove our inner child into hiding. Yet, the child inside holds the key to living fully human lives in the present. Our childhood trauma is often stored in our minds, bodies, and spirits, waiting to be released when the time is right. We understand that grief is cumulative, which means all the abuse, neglect, and shaming we experienced in our past are piled up. We had not forgotten them as we had thought. As we re-experience our inner child's truth and feel the memories of the past, the tears of grieving and healing will come.

As adult children, our core wounds are shame and abandonment. Shame tramples a child's natural love and trust, and replaces it with fear and self-doubt. With shame, we lost our ability to trust ourselves or others. To shame a child IS to abandon the child. The dilemma of abandonment is a choice between painful attempts at intimacy and hopeless isolation. Either way, the results are the same: We live our lives deprived of warmth and love, trying to protect ourselves by rejecting and abandoning our vulnerable child within.

Protective aspects of us may also emerge through the reparenting process and can have destructive tendencies. This is a paradox of sorts. While the child within is our original wholeness who believed in people and freely gave love and trust, this child can also store hurt, pain, and loss. Some see the adaptive, angry, and aggressive aspects of ourselves as an inner teenager. Fortunately, our younger parts inside us will listen if our loving parent gently and patiently builds trust with them. Inner parts work can be tender and humorous, and it can be volatile and unsettling. This is why we do this with others. With support from our fellow travelers, we learn to use the ACA reparenting techniques (p.30) to safely connect with our younger selves.

Through reparenting, we discover that love dissolves shame. We give ourselves the love we seek by embracing our child (or children) inside. Connected to our inner child's sensitivity and curiosity, we rise and reach out to explore the world anew. By accepting and reuniting with our vulnerable inner child, we begin to heal the broken pieces of our shattered selves, and become whole, conscious human beings … joyfully engaging the world with natural confidence, love, and trust.

Chapter 8
QUESTIONS

1. How do I feel about the idea of having an inner child? Am I more comfortable with terms such as "younger self" or "little one?" What works best for me?

2. Some adult children practice quietly sitting still (meditating) to listen to their child inside. What happens when I quietly sit still for short periods?

3. Some ACAs use a body scan to connect with their inner kids "speaking" to them. What do I notice as I focus (in order) on my head, face, neck, shoulders, arms, hands, chest, back, stomach, groin, legs, & feet that can tell me how I'm feeling?

4. What does the wounded part of me (inner child) need to hear from the inner, caring part of myself (loving parent) to feel safe, supported, and comforted?

5. What does the protective part of me (inner teenager) need to hear from the caring part of myself (loving parent) to feel heard, validated, and respected?

CHAPTER 8 OPTIONAL FURTHER READING:
ACA Big Red Book
- Chapter 8: section; "ACA Experience …" testimonials (pp.309–326)
- Chapter 8: section; "Chapter 8 Exercises" (pgs.328–330)

ACA Strengthening My Recovery (Daily Affirmations)
- June 19, p.177 – "Non-Dominant Hand"
- September 9, p.262 – "Inner Child"

The Loving Parent Guidebook
- Chapter 6: "Discovering Your Inner Teenager" (p.63)
- Chapter 6: "Discovering Your Inner Child" (p.76)

Chapter 8
INNER CHILD SUPPLEMENT

ACA Reparenting Techniques
(adapted from BRB Ch. 8, pp. 304–306)

- Willingness—even if reparenting seems strange, we're open to giving it a try
- Journaling, non-dominant handwriting, introductory letters
- Guided meditations, visualizations, other types of meditation
- Looking through childhood photos (or writing/drawing/talking about them)
- Drawing, painting, sketching, doodling
- Listening to music or dancing; other forms of expressive movement
- Meditative physical movement such as gentle stretching (yoga, qigong)
- Use of affirmations as the voice of the inner loving parent
- Evoking memories through the senses (sight, hearing, taste, touch, smell)
- Mirror work
- ACA Reparenting Check-in (The Loving Parent Guidebook, Chapter 9, p.94)

Mirror Work*
(Adapted from BRB Ch. 15, "Beyond Survival: Practicing Self-Love." For additional mirror work exercises, see "The Loving Parent Guidebook" Chapter 15, p.157)

Find a quiet place with a mirror large enough to show your face and shoulders. Stare quietly at your image in the mirror and remain still while noticing any feelings, thoughts, or words that arise. Look at your hair, forehead, lips, throat, chin, and so on. Notice your posture. Notice your breathing. Be aware of any body sensations you experience in your head, throat, chest, stomach, and abdomen. If you choose, you can keep a notepad nearby to write about this experience. Some adult children describe doing this exercise as "listening to" the child within. As you do this exercise, ask yourself if it is your inner critical parent* or loving parent who "listens?"

Next, look into your own eyes and repeat some of the reparenting affirmations that begin with, "It's OK."—"It's OK to trust. It's OK not to know. It's OK to feel angry. It's OK to ask for help. It's OK to say no. It's OK to cry. It's OK to dream and have hope." You can also try using other affirmations if you have discovered some that work well for you. Note your feelings, thoughts, and body sensations. Some adult children describe this exercise as their loving parent learning to "speak to" the child within.

---

* Note: if your inner critical parent is active during this exercise, you may need to set an internal limit or boundary with that part of you. If it gets too intense, you can take a gentleness break, or contact a trusted fellow traveler for support.

Chapter 8
INNER CHILD SUPPLEMENT

An ACA Inner Child Guided Meditation Exercise
(Excerpted from BRB Chapter 7, "The Twelve Steps of ACA," section "Step Eleven.")

You can use this exercise to connect with your inner child. Consider reading and record the script below in your own voice. When ready to begin the exercise, find a quiet location and sit upright but comfortably on the ground or chair. Close your eyes. Take a few deep breaths. Come to a place of relaxation and breathe naturally. Begin playback of the recording. When finished, consider journaling, writing, or drawing about what you felt and heard from your child within, or about the experience. If at any point this exercise gets too intense, you can take a gentleness break, or reach out to a trusted fellow traveler.

[START SCRIPT] Imagine that you are sitting on a warm beach. The weather is pleasant and not too hot. The beach is secluded but safe. You can feel the warm sand beneath your feet as you stand up and look out upon a calm, blue ocean. White seagulls are diving for fish, and the smell of seawater is refreshing. In front of you, near the shoreline, you see an image of yourself when you were six or eight years old. Your inner child is picking up starfish and seashells. The child notices you and waves you over. You walk up to the child, and the child reaches out and places a starfish in one of your hands. You smile and feel the bristles of the tiny starfish tickling you. Your inner child smiles and squints to block the friendly sun.

The child reaches out and grips your hand. The child's skin has been warmed by sun rays. You both begin walking along the beach. You notice the child's soft hair and sensitive touch as you stroll. The child trusts you and giggles softly each time a wave washes up the shore, almost touching your feet. You walk for many moments, chatting softly, but paying attention to the child's innocence and imagination. You want to protect the child.

You notice two people ahead, and they seem familiar, so you keep walking toward them. Your inner child squeezes your hand and moves slightly behind you as you move closer to the people. The child becomes shy, pushing into your leg from behind. You keep walking. You recognize the couple as your parents, waiting for you to walk up. They grin at you and your inner child. They ask if they can walk with the child. You feel your stomach tighten, and you look down at your inner child to find the child pressed into your legs from the back. The child won't look at you and won't let go of your hand. You smile at your parents but ask them to wait for another day to walk with the child. You and your inner child walk up the beach away from your parents and sit down.

The child looks over a shoulder and sits in your lap. You hold your inner child. You both watch your parents walk away. The sun is lower now but still warm. Your inner child naps, and you both are safe. You are going to make it. You are learning new ways of being as your inner loving parent strengthens. You can trust yourself to take care of your inner child. You can trust yourself to love. [END SCRIPT]

Chapter 9
TWELVE STEPS IN ACA ACA TWELVE STEPS / TONY A's STEPS

Since their original publication by AA in 1939, the Twelve Steps have relieved the suffering of millions dealing with alcoholism, drug abuse, codependency, and many other addictions, obsessions, and compulsions.

The ACA 12 Steps differ slightly from the original 12 Steps. Additionally, ACA co-founder, Tony A., developed a variation of the Steps that resonates with some ACA members. Along with reparenting, the ACA 12 Steps are an essential part of ACA recovery. Adult children usually work the Steps using the yellow workbook, 12 Steps of Adult Children, either with a sponsor or another fellow traveler, or as part of studies or workgroups. The purpose of the ACA 12 Steps is to uncover the truth of our childhood wounding, and to recover from the effects of childhood trauma.

Beginning with Step 1, we address denial. This can involve refusing to admit that abuse or neglect occurred in our childhood—or denying the effects of childhood harms in our adult lives. We confront the truths of powerlessness and unmanageability. Denial about our childhood wounding was reinforced through the rules of family dysfunction: "Don't talk–Don't trust–Don't feel." Breaking these rules helps us break through our denial.

Moving to Steps 2 & 3, we confront issues of faith and higher or greater power—challenging and sensitive topics for some of us. We remember ACA is a spiritual, not a religious program. We are each free to discover what supports us in our efforts to release some control in our lives. In Steps 4 & 5, we review in detail how we were raised. ACA Step 4, in particular, is quite different than in other 12 Step programs. In ACA, we examine our parents' behavior, family roles, messages, rules, abuse, neglect, and how these things affect us as adults. We seek a full remembrance so that we can start to grieve our childhood losses.

In Steps 6 & 7, we recognize our outdated survival mechanisms and begin to release them. In Steps 8 & 9, we seek self-forgiveness, and make amends to ourselves and others as appropriate. Steps 10 through 12 focus on self-love and maintaining a healthy way of life in recovery.

For the beginner in ACA, the journey starts with Step 1. The ACA program will unfold over time, bringing rich rewards of self-acceptance and emotional sobriety. We suggest that ACA members work the Steps in order, not looking ahead to avoid becoming overwhelmed. We approach the Steps gently, with patience and respect, as we learn to become our own loving parent ... one step at a time.

Chapter 9
QUESTIONS

1. If this is my first exposure to the 12 Steps, what is my impression? If I have been in other 12 Step programs, how might working the ACA 12 Steps differ? What is my impression of Tony A's 12 Steps compared to the ACA 12 Steps (pp.76–77)?

2. How have addiction and compulsion played a role in my life? How might these behaviors be connected to the dysfunction I experienced in my childhood?

3. In what ways have I experienced overpowering obsession with another human being that causes me to deny my own needs or neglect my own self-care?

4. Have I ignored my feelings of shame, fear, and neglect to survive my childhood? If so, how have I been able to do that?

5. How might I bring ACA reparenting (becoming my own loving parent) into my ACA 12 Step recovery work?

CHAPTER 9 OPTIONAL FURTHER READING:
ACA Big Red Book
- Chapter 7 – "The 12 Steps of ACA: Part 1" (pp. 91–117)

ACA Strengthening My Recovery (Daily Affirmations)
- January 5, p.6 – "Acting Purposefully"
- January 22, p.23 – "Step Four"
- March 25, p.88 – "Disease of Alcoholism
- July 8, p.197 – "Willingness"

Chapter 10
STEP 1 INTRODUCTION

ACA Step 1: "Admitted we were powerless over the effects of alcoholism or other family dysfunction, that our lives had become unmanageable."

In Step 1, we acknowledge that our family upbringing was dysfunctional, and that we carried the painful effects of that childhood wounding into our adult lives. We become more aware of intergenerational trauma. The spiritual principles of this first Step are powerlessness, unmanageability, and surrender.

Many adult children struggle with the notion of powerlessness. However, the powerlessness we describe in ACA Step 1 differs from the learned helplessness we experienced as children. As children, we couldn't leave our homes when we feared for our safety. Trapped, we may even have come to believe we deserved the pain we encountered. We developed stories that minimized our parents' abusive and neglectful behavior. We created an inner critical parent to help us avoid unfair treatment. As children, we figured out ways to survive. And inevitably, we brought those survival skills into adulthood as the Laundry List and Other Laundry List Traits. In Step 1, we discover we were powerless over this inescapable progression.

Next, we come to realize that relying on our childhood survival Traits creates unmanageability. As adult children, we fear authority figures, or we can become harsh authority figures in other people's lives. We people-please; we judge ourselves harshly; we feel guilty when we stand up for ourselves. We confuse love and pity and tend to "love" people we can rescue or control, while yearning for others to rescue us. Through Step 1, we recognize that what we once thought to be "manageability" was actually white-knuckling attempts at control. However, asking us to surrender control is like asking us to jump from an airplane without a parachute—terrifying and seemingly impossible.

In ACA, surrender involves letting go, asking for help, and then accepting the support offered. Some adult children speak of this place as "hitting an emotional bottom." Others describe surrender as finally acknowledging a wounded child within. By surrendering, we give up the notion that we can reason out a solution alone or that we can avoid discomfort in the healing process. We release the illusion we must be in control to continue hiding our shame. We accept our inability to change the past and our powerlessness to control the future. We are then left with real life in the present. In ACA Step 1, we pass through a threshold where hope, healing, and a new way of life are possible.

Chapter 10
QUESTIONS

1. How is experiencing powerlessness as an adult different from how we experienced helplessness as a child? What am I powerless over today?

2. In what ways have I acted helpless as an adult when in reality, I was manipulating others to get what I thought I needed?

3. How have I used food, sex, drugs, alcohol, work, porn, electronics, relationships, or other addictive/compulsive behaviors to an extreme? Have I felt powerless over these activities? How have these things made my life unmanageable?

4. Which of the Laundry List or Other List Traits has contributed most to unmanageability in my life (pp.68–69)?

5. What does "surrender" mean to me? What am I scared will happen if I let go? How might I benefit by letting go or surrendering?

CHAPTER 10 OPTIONAL FURTHER READING:

ACA Big Red Book
- Chapter 7: "The 12 Steps of ACA: Part 1" (pp.96–106)
- Chapter 7: "The 12 Steps of ACA: Part 2 – Step 1" (pp.118–129)

ACA Strengthening My Recovery (Daily Affirmations)
- January 3, p.4 – "Step One"
- September 1, p.254 – "Surrender"
- September 22, p.275 – "Step One"
- October 25, p.309 – "Control"

Chapter 11
SPIRITUALITY

In some ways, ACA might look and feel like a religious program because the Twelve Steps, and much of our program literature, include such words as "God" and "prayer." However, ACA leaves matters of faith and belief up to the individual. In ACA, we honor every member's freedom to believe or not believe as they wish. Atheists, agnostics, and believers are all welcome and valued in ACA.

ACA is a spiritual program that examines all the effects of family dysfunction, including our relationship to, or the absence of, power(s) greater than ourselves. Frankly, some of us struggle with this part of the program. However, knowing where our understanding of a higher power today originated from and exploring these beliefs is a critical part of our healing.

Some adult children have assigned the characteristics of their dysfunctional parents to a higher power. If their parents were shaming, vengeful, and inconsistent, for example, then their higher power tends to be the same. Some adult children recall praying for their abuse to stop, but nothing changed. They wonder, "How can a higher power allow small children to be treated so ruthlessly?" Other adult children are staunch believers but use their higher power and religion as tools of control. Some are former believers who think they have been abandoned and cannot reclaim faith in any type of higher power. In ACA, we learn to become our own loving parent and see our biological parents as "instruments of our existence." Doing so can release our parents as role models for something greater than ourselves. The ACA Solution states: "Our actual parent is our higher power." As we heal, some of us come to believe this statement literally, others perhaps more figuratively.

At its core, spirituality itself is a process of surrender: We release the illusion that we alone must have all the answers. When we recognize that we need help and sincerely ask for it in our ACA community, we open to sources of love, healing, acceptance, and wisdom that we never knew existed. To our amazement, these resources become increasingly accessible, and our world becomes bigger and kinder. Some of us explain this in secular terms, such as the power of friendship, community, and connection. Others speak of nature, the universe, or life itself. And still others more comfortably describe these resources in traditionally religious language. But whether atheist, agnostic, or believer ... all recovering adult children have access to something greater than themselves. In this sense, spirituality is what many of us feel sitting among fellow travelers at an ACA meeting, and experience within as we learn to become our own loving parents.

Chapter 11
QUESTIONS

1. What do I remember being told as a child about faith, belief, prayer, and a higher power?

2. In what ways does my view of higher power (or "reality") resemble how I view my parents (harsh, indifferent, distant, abandoning, etc.)?

3. What "powers" might there be that are greater than my false self?

4. Am I open to the idea that I have had an inner strength all along that helped me survive a dysfunctional childhood? If so, how do I describe that inner strength?

5. Do I believe I can love myself (my inner child)? Do I believe it's OK to ask for help? What resources do I have today that I didn't have in my childhood?

CHAPTER 11 OPTIONAL FURTHER READING:

ACA Big Red Book
- Chapter 5 – "ACA is a Spiritual Not Religious Program" (p.75)
- Chapter 7 – "The Twelve Steps of ACA," Part 1, section: "Examining Spiritual Beliefs" (pp. 106–108)

ACA Strengthening My Recovery (Daily Affirmations)
- April 14, p.109 – "Higher Power
- July 13, p.202 – "Spiritual, not Religious"
- July 26, p.215 – "Step Two"
- November 18, p.334 – "Personal Higher Power"

Chapter 12
CHILDHOOD TRAUMA

In times of danger, children run home for safety. But where do kids run when danger is within the home … when their caregivers are absent, neglectful, or even the cause of stress, pain, and abuse? The natural responses to danger are fight, flight, or freeze. Most of us as children could not fight or run—so we froze: We froze, and we hid within.

Childhood trauma affects adult children in body, mind, and spirit long after leaving the dysfunctional home. A lifetime of pushing down and holding back injury and hurt from consciousness can be agonizing. Many of us have painful physical and emotional symptoms, debilitating anxiety, obsessive thoughts, and compulsive behaviors that often seem unexplainable. A common diagnosis used today for those suffering from childhood trauma is Post Traumatic Stress Disorder (PTSD, or complex/C-PTSD).

Many of us as children learned to repress our feelings or memories as a protection mechanism. If asked today what happened to us as kids, we may have defining moments that we can recall, but we might also have years of "blanks." We may question what we do remember or why we can't attach any feelings to specific memories. Some of us have been so traumatized that we shut down our emotions, cut ourselves off from our bodies, and "check out." We may outwardly appear as fully functioning adults, but we are dissociated.

In ACA, we learn trauma does not go away until we address the original wounds: As we feel, we will heal. We learn to "reconnect" with our bodies and grow in our ability to be present. But it can be difficult for many of us to understand what our body is trying to tell us. To survive, we taught ourselves to ignore our body and feelings, and thus, we can misinterpret its language. Our wounding goes deep, though—it's in our blood, tissue, nerves, and bone. Our bodies "remember" what happened, so we begin to listen. We turn within to re-discover our truths … painful as the process may be.

As we learn to become our own loving parent, our frozen, hidden inner child can safely re-emerge, and we begin to free ourselves. We feel anger at those who harmed us, and at others who stood by and did nothing. We hit pillows and scream if we have to, but we no longer hold it all in. We connect to the terror we blocked out as vulnerable children, and it slowly loosens its grip on us. We share our story and listen to others: We talk, we trust, and we feel. We discover we weren't the cause of what happened, and we let go of blaming ourselves. We feel sadness and grieve all that was lost, and in doing so, discover all that can yet be.

Chapter 12
QUESTIONS

1. What physical symptoms have I experienced that may be related to trauma, such as: Headaches; racing heart & shortness of breath; muscle tension, body aches & pains, sharp or dull sensations; stomach problems, nausea, vomiting, diarrhea; genital pain or numbness; strange tastes or a lump in the throat?

2. What emotional symptoms have I experienced that may be related to trauma, such as: Hopelessness; absence of emotion; irritability or agitation; mood swings; anxiety; panic or confusion; insomnia or nightmares; disorientation when stressed; hypervigilance for potential threats; being easily startled?

3. What addictions, obsessions, or compulsive behaviors have I experienced that may be related to trauma, such as: Alcohol or drug abuse; co-dependency; issues with food, sex, shopping, gambling, etc.; intrusive/repetitive thoughts; excessive counting, tapping, checking on things; strange habits, rituals & routines?

4. How open am I to the idea that some of these "hard to explain," often painful difficulties I experience in adulthood may be related to childhood trauma?

CHAPTER 12 OPTIONAL FURTHER READING:
ACA Big Red Book
- Introduction – "The Doctor's Opinion" (p. xxvii)
- Chapter 2 – "It Will Never Happen To Me (Abuse & Neglect)" (pp.21–34)
- Chapter 7 – "Post-Traumatic Stress Disorder" (pp.177–182)

ACA Strengthening My Recovery (Daily Affirmations)
- July 18, p.207 – "Stored Trauma"
- August 22, p.243 – "PTSD"

Chapter 13
GRIEF

By gradually releasing the burden of unexpressed grief, we slowly move out of the past. We learn to reparent ourselves with gentleness, humor, love, and respect.
—ACA Solution

The grief we speak of in ACA is our cumulative childhood loss. Grief is the built-up defeats and disappointments we experienced through our family's abusive actions and neglectful inaction. The lack of unconditional love from our caregivers robbed us of our ability to feel whole. Burdened with shame, we lost trust in ourselves and others. We carried these fundamental losses of connection into our adult lives.

The Laundry Lists Traits kept us busy, distracted, and numbed, but we could never really escape the pain of our childhood trauma. If we sought help, our unexpressed grief was usually diagnosed as depression and commonly treated with temporary remedies. We learn in ACA that instead of masking our symptoms, we need to feel our sadness to release our stored grief. There is a difference between the stagnant quality of hopelessness in being depressed, and the flowing quality of restorative grief work. Depression seems like a permanent, stuck state … it drags us down and makes us feel like there's no way out. Grief work involves movement towards acceptance, integration, clarity, and peace.

We indirectly address our childhood losses each time we attend an ACA meeting and listen to the experiences of other adult children. Sharing the burden of grief others feel gives us the courage and strength to face our own bereavement. We can journal about childhood incidents to help us loosen our "stuffed" feelings. If they don't surface, we can imagine how any other child would feel in our situation. We can also look at our childhood photos. Pictures can awaken our emotions and bring memories into focus. When we connect with our inner child, we rediscover our innocence and truth.

Before ACA recovery, many adult children eventually stopped crying because their tears did not bring relief from the relentless despair and abandonment wounds. Grief work restores the power of tears. With support from our fellow travelers, we cry deeply, knowing that we are finally safe and understood. By finding our grief, we come to believe on a deeper level that our parents' dysfunction was not our fault. We did not do anything wrong as children to cause them to harm us. We never were deficient or defective. Through ACA reparenting, we eventually speak of grief with a sense of serenity rather than sorrow or resentment. We make peace with our losses and find wholeness.

Chapter 13
QUESTIONS

1. When have I experienced loss as an adult? How did I react to those losses?

2. Think of a situation when a family member shamed, abused, or neglected you as a child. What did I not receive as a child in that situation that I would have received in a healthy family? (This is a way to measure our loss.)

3. Some adult children say that while they knew the dysfunction in their childhood was not their fault, a part of them always FELT like and believed they were to blame. How might this statement relate to my grieving process?

4. What words can my loving parent use to help my inner child work through the feelings that arise through grieving (fear, anger, sadness, other feelings)?

5. How does grieving allow me to break the rules of family dysfunction, "Don't talk, trust, or feel?" How can trusted fellow travelers support my grief work?

CHAPTER 13 OPTIONAL FURTHER READING:
ACA Big Red Book
- Chapter 7, Step 5: "Grief: The Onion and Time," "What to Expect in Addressing Grief," and "Pinpointing and Measuring Loss/Grief" (pp.199–204)

ACA Strengthening My Recovery (Daily Affirmations)
- February 19, p. 52 – "Isolation and Grieving"
- June 23, p. 212 – "Grief and Childhood"
- December 21, p. 368 – "Stuck Grief"

Chapter 14
RELATIONSHIPS

In our dysfunctional childhood homes, we learned to shut down our natural need for connection: *We disconnected to protect our hearts.* The soul rupture of our early wounding instilled a desperate sense of abandonment and aloneness. As we grew older, we began our lifelong quest ... looking externally for love and safety that never comes.

Adult children can appear outwardly confident, but we carry the same fear, shame, and self-doubt we picked up in childhood. We ignore red flags, enduring one unhealthy relationship after the next—painfully trying to fill the hole inside that can't be filled. The "withdrawal" from our dysfunctional relationships can be just as agonizing as an addict's withdrawal from drugs. What many adult children described as love before reaching ACA was actually codependence or rigid control. If we did try to "love" others, we did so while trapped in the Laundry Lists Traits, or lost in our addictions and fears. Some adult children experience relationship anorexia, choosing emotional isolation over vulnerability with others altogether.

When we begin to unconditionally love and accept our true self, we become capable of having healthy relationships with others. Intimate connection begins by embracing the child inside—backfilling the love and nurturing we did not receive as children. With our loving parent guiding us, we rediscover our feelings, wants, and needs. We learn to walk away from the craziness that once confused and trapped us.

Our ACA fellow travelers can help us learn and practice new relationship skills, sharing their experience, strength, and hope and how they relate to our struggles and successes. They can be a mirror for us, reflecting back what they hear us say. They can help us identify when we're caught in the critical parent's distorted thinking, and explore ways to create breathing room. They can model their loving parent voice for us when ours is shaky or distant. As we learn to trust others and directly ask for the support we need, our inner loving parent grows stronger, and our emerging inner child feels safer.

With patience and practice, we take our ACA recovery into the world. All our relationships can be different—friendship, work, family, and even romantic partnerships. We choose to bring people into our lives who have healthy boundaries and who can be responsible for themselves. We become willing to share our true self with others who can love responsibly in return. As adult children, we have lived a life of disconnection for too long. With support from ACA, our internal intimacy translates into outward connection, and we become fully human.

Chapter 14
QUESTIONS

1. BRB Chapter 13 states: "A healthy relationship involves talking about feelings, mutual respect, and a commitment to trust and honesty." How did the "Don't talk –Don't trust–Don't feel" rules set me up for troubled relationships?

2. When have I experienced the pain of my childhood abandonment wounds in my adult relationships, believing at that time that I was being "abandoned?"

3. How have other people's feelings, thoughts, or reactions influenced or even determined my behavior and choices? How does this relate to codependence?

4. In what ways might "manageability" in my life have actually been controlling behavior with others that I mislabeled? How does this relate to codependence?

5. How can having a healthy connection with myself (my inner child) and other fellow travelers lead to healthier family, work, and romantic relationships? How might this differ from codependence?

CHAPTER 14 OPTIONAL FURTHER READING:

ACA Big Red Book
- Chapter 13: "Relationships: Applying What We Have Learned" (p.401)
- Chapter 14: "Taking Our Program to Work" (p.415)

ACA Strengthening My Recovery (Daily Affirmations)
- January 6, p.7 – "Abusive Relationships"
- March 8, p.71 – "Intimacy"
- July 14, p.208 – "Using Others"

Chapter 15
FELLOW TRAVELERS

In our dysfunctional home environments, we learned not to talk or feel … and we learned not to trust. In the absence of trust, many adult children developed a fear of authority in childhood (Traits 1 & 3), a desire to seek approval from those in authority (Trait 2), or reflexive reactions to fight against authority (Other Traits). Some of us tried to protect ourselves by using the power of authority and control against others (Other Traits). Perhaps we feared in ACA that we would find ourselves in similar unhealthy, exhausting relationships. Caught between the pain of isolation and paralyzing indecision, we may have wondered how we would ever learn to safely trust other people.

Connecting with **fellow travelers** in ACA can be a courageous first step in opening to intimacy with others. As we bring our inner child into our lives, trusting another person with our most vulnerable selves can feel new and scary. We learn to trust others gradually and allow others to do the same. When we connect with fellow travelers, it may be the first emotionally honest relationship we have ever had. We learn to ask for what we need honestly rather than use manipulation. We learn to communicate respectfully, follow through on commitments, and forgive in ways we were never taught, and perhaps believed impossible.

As we seek out support and offer help to others in our ACA recovery connections, we avoid taking responsibility for one another's recovery: We don't try to be a therapist, counselor, life coach, guru, or "parent" for anyone else—nor can we expect others to serve these roles in our healing process. The ACA Solution is to become our own loving parent. We share our experience, strength, and hope with one another … seeking answers and solutions together. We help each other understand program principles, language, and concepts. We encourage each other with reparenting work, Step work, and use of other program tools, techniques, and resources. Our most trusted fellow travelers support us in learning to feel our feelings deeply, to discover our authentic wants and needs, and to speak our truth and set boundaries. In our fellowship, we hold space for each other as we break the old rules of family dysfunction: Don't talk—Don't trust—Don't feel.

In ACA, we explore a diversity of supportive relationships within the framework of communal recovery. Some work with a sponsor, and some work with one or more fellow travelers. Regardless of our approach, ACA encourages us to create healthy support networks. We must come out of isolation to bring trust into our lives. We embrace the paradox that while no other person can do our recovery work for us, none of us can heal alone.

Chapter 15
QUESTIONS

1. When I asked for help as a child, what responses did I get? How might that affect my willingness to seek out support from others today?

2. When in adulthood have I had an over-reliance on others for direction, answers, and approval? How do I feel when I try to make another person my "parent?"

3. When have I tried to manage another person's life? How do I feel when I have taken on the role of "parent" for another adult?

4. In what ways can a recovery partner support me to become my OWN loving parent without taking on the role of becoming my "parent?"

5. What benefits might there be in seeking support and encouragement from a network of trusted fellow travelers (see next page)?

CHAPTER 15 OPTIONAL FURTHER READING:
ACA Big Red Book
- Chapter 11: "ACA Sponsorship: Fellow Travelers" (p.365)

Trifold Brochures
- ACA Sponsorship: Fellow Travelers

ACA Strengthening My Recovery (Daily Affirmations)
- January 1, p.2 – "Fellow Travelers"
- January 26, p.27 – "Sponsorship"
- March 16, p.79 – "Fear of Authority"
- July 2, p.191 – "Asking for Help"

Chapter 15
FELLOW TRAVELERS SUPPLEMENT

Building Trustworthy Connections in ACA
We seek to connect with other ACA fellow travelers who ...

- can be supportive of us in our ACA reparenting/recovery work.
- can be responsible for their own reparenting/recovery and own boundaries.
- can be honest with themselves and others.
- can be accountable by following through on commitments.
- can be respectful by refraining from harsh judgment and personal criticism.
- can, if needed, utilize outside resources for directive accountability with their primary addictions, compulsions, and obsessions, or other acting out behaviors.

We try to interact with others in these same trustworthy ways.

Fellow Traveler Aspirations
As we do our ACA reparenting/recovery work and heal our Laundry Lists Traits behaviors, we seek to interact with others in healthier ways:

- I can ask for help—I am not a burden.
- I can know when to offer help—I am not obligated.
- I can be open to others' experience, strength, and hope without seeking advice.
- I can share my experience, strength, and hope instead of giving advice.
- I can refrain from trying to please others I want to impress.
- I can refrain from trying to intimidate others into seeking my approval.
- I can avoid trying to find others to fix, save, or rescue me.
- I can avoid trying to fix, save, or rescue others.
- I can learn from others without making them an all-knowing authority.
- I can share with others without thinking I am an all-knowing authority.
- I can be free from the burdens of inferiority and grandiosity.
- I can be equal in relationships with other people.
- I can say yes when I want/need to and no when I want/need to.
- I can maintain healthy boundaries.
- I can be capable of selecting healthy people with whom to work my program.

Chapter 15
FELLOW TRAVELERS CONTACTS

Chapter 16
SERVICE

We were each born with a true self which allows us to be sensitive and present for others. Tragically, childhood wounding could turn our inherent gifts into the Laundry Lists Traits … expressions of a false self. Our natural empathy was distorted into caretaking and rescuing; our willingness to cooperate turned into people-pleasing; and our desire to help others could easily manifest as codependent control. We became overly responsible or shut people out completely. We learned to focus on others, and in the process abandon ourselves.

The essence of service in ACA is action coming from love. But to truly serve one another in healthy, loving ways, we must first be willing to love and serve our true self. Our initial act of service in ACA was walking through the door of our first meeting—an incredibly courageous act of self-love. We continue to love and serve ourselves as we "keep coming back" and when we talk, trust, and feel. When we share at meetings, our courage to connect with our true self naturally encourages others to do the same, and we are being of service.

As we patiently practice reparenting in ACA, we learn to gently attune to our child within. By learning to connect deeply with our true self, we become increasingly available to support others, too. We more easily put down our phones, make eye contact longer, and fidget and daydream less. We practice the art of "holding space" and being a "witness" for our fellow travelers in their healing. We watch for our Laundry Lists Traits behaviors to arise through our false self expressions. We become better able to discern if our helping and giving is in alignment with the ACA Solution. We ask, "Does my approach to being of service right now support me and my fellow travelers in becoming our own loving parents?"

As we continue to heal and step out of isolation, we might choose to arrive at a meeting early, serve as a greeter, or stay afterward to help clean up. With continued recovery in ACA, we may chair a meeting, serve as the group secretary or treasurer, or even start a new ACA group one day. Eventually, we come to understand that service is not only an expression of self-love, but potentially a way to give thanks. We can give back to help ensure that the rooms of ACA recovery continue to be available for ourselves and others. Being of service also allows us to work through remaining Traits and unhealthy behaviors in new ways.

In 12 Step programs we commonly hear, "We must give away what we have to keep it." However, in ACA, we also learn that to go outward and help others in healthy ways, we must first turn inward to connect with our true self.

Chapter 16
QUESTIONS

1. What did I learn in childhood about my role in addressing other people's needs? How might that role have related to getting my own needs met as a child?

2. When in adulthood have I focused on others at the expense of my well-being?

3. What Laundry Lists Traits (pp.68–69) tend to come up for me when helping others and giving of myself?

4. Some adult children worry about feeling obligated or being trapped when considering being of service. Others think they don't have much value to offer. What concerns do I have when it comes to being of service or helping others?

5. How might connecting with my inner child help me be of service in healthy ways, both to others and myself?

CHAPTER 16 OPTIONAL FURTHER READING:
ACA Big Red Book
- Chapter 10: "The Importance of Service in ACA" (p.353)
- Chapter 19: "The Twelve Traditions of ACA"

ACA Strengthening My Recovery (Daily Affirmations)
- March 18, p.81 – "Service"
- July 27, p.216 – "Codependence"
- September 11, p.264 – "Spiritual Experience"
- September 13, p.266 – "Service"

Chapter 17
ACA PROMISES

Adult children can grow up promising themselves: "I will never be like my parents — it will never happen to me." Yet rarely are we able to keep that promise. In ACA, we rediscover the child within and open to new promises of healing. Our ability to feel deepens; our ability to recall sharpens. As we heal and become more integrated, we find greater connection within ourselves and with others. After having been fragmented for so long in so many ways, we *awaken to a sense of wholeness we never knew was possible.*

The **ACA Promises** and Flip Sides of the Laundry Lists describe what can happen as we reconnect with our true self, and learn to work with our false self in new ways. For many adult children, reparenting involves integration—a process of *reclaiming, transforming,* and *releasing* towards greater wholeness. Some describe integration as walking into the shadows of our being and getting to know ourselves more deeply. In doing so, we encounter our core shame and abandonment wounds, and we discover what may be our greatest challenge—trust. With gentleness and patience, we reunite with our inner child and *reclaim* greater wholeness. We grieve our losses, and in time, we find forgiveness and a greater sense of freedom.

Along this path, we also encounter our adaptive false self aspects such as people-pleasing, confusing love with pity, and judging ourselves harshly. Initially, these protective parts of us may provoke fear or anger. With the voice of our loving parent instead of the inner critic, we bring these parts of ourselves into greater consciousness. These survival Traits kept us alive as kids, but they no longer serve us in ways they once did. Eventually, these parts of ourselves *transform* for our benefit, and we release that which restricts our recovery. In time, we come to feel more at peace.

ACA recovery is not necessarily an easy path, nor is it a solitary event. At times, it can be scary, and we will have doubts. But to heal dysfunction in our lives, we must pause our running away and instead turn inward. The ACA Solution is reparenting—*to become our own loving parent.* The ACA 12 Steps, our fellow travelers, and powers greater than ourselves can all help anchor and support us on this journey. Many of us come to discover that when our inner child is in the loving and protective embrace of our inner loving parent, there is nothing "out there" that threatens us "in here." Through our own internal intimacy and wholeness, we find safe connection with others and the world around us. As we *talk, trust,* and *feel,* we find **a new hope**, and we bring the Promises of ACA recovery and serenity into our lives.

Chapter 17
QUESTIONS

1. What promises did I make to myself in childhood about how my life would be as an adult?

2. What parts of myself have I discovered in my recovery process? What ACA reparenting techniques (p.30) am I using to reclaim and heal those parts?

3. What ACA tools of recovery (p.18) have I been using to support my healing journey?

4. How does my inner loving parent support me to move to the flip sides of the Laundry Lists Traits (pp.70–73)?

5. What ACA Promises (p.79) am I starting to see come true in my life?

CHAPTER 17 OPTIONAL FURTHER READING:
ACA Big Red Book
- Chapter 6: "ACA – How It Works" (p.81)
- Chapter 15: "Beyond Survival" – section, "The ACA Promises" (pp. 442–443)

The Laundry Lists Workbook: Integrating Our Laundry Lists Traits
- Traits 1–14 introductory pages, sections "Flip Sides of the Laundry Lists"

ACA Strengthening My Recovery (Daily Affirmations)
- June 9, p.72 – "Freedom"
- April 2, p.97 – "Wholeness"
- November 11, p.327 – "Serenity"

Chapter 17
EXTRA SPACE FOR SOMETHING FUN

Chapter 17
EXTRA SPACE FOR SOMETHING FUN

APPENDICES

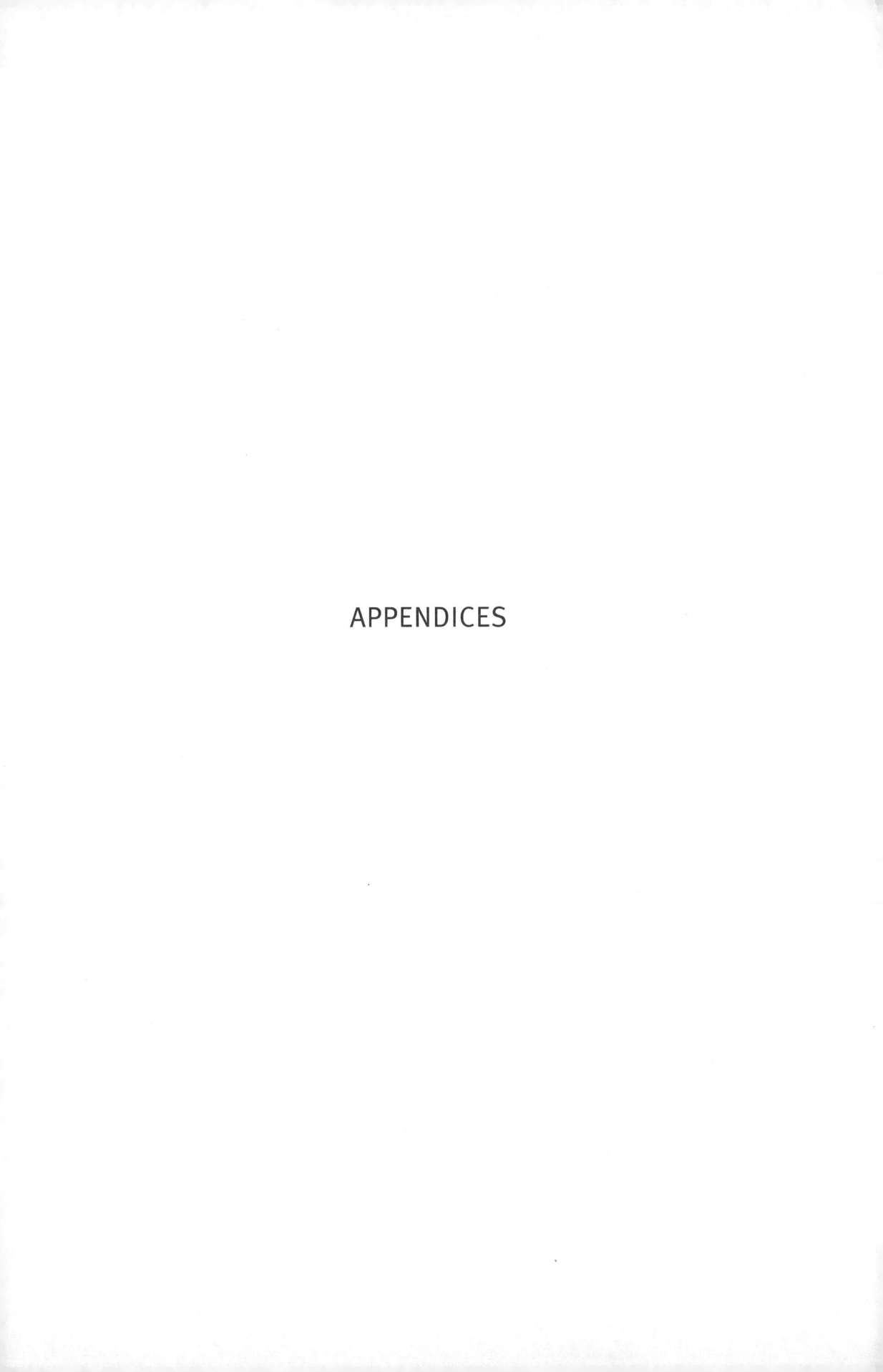

Appendix A
SAMPLE MEETING FORMAT

Meeting Opening Format

Hello. My name is _____. Welcome to [GROUP NAME] BEGINNER'S MEETING of Adult Children of Alcoholic and Dysfunctional Families. At this time, please silence all electronic devices.

At ACA, we meet to share the experience we had as children growing up in dysfunctional homes, and how that experience affects us in our adult lives today. Dysfunctional homes often, but not always, include alcoholism or other forms of drug abuse. Family dysfunction can also occur in rigidly religious, militaristic, or punitive homes—or homes dominated by control, harsh judgment, & perfectionism. Any type of abuse or neglect creates dysfunctional home environments, as can parental mental illness or other forms of parental disability. Persistent debt or gambling can be other signs of family dysfunction. Those adopted, raised in foster care, or raised in single-parent homes may also find healing in ACA.

1. Will all those who care to, please join me in the ACA Serenity Prayer?
2. Will a friend please read The Laundry List or The Problem?
3. Will a friend please read The Solution?
4. Will a friend please read one of the versions of the 12 Steps ... ACA or Tony A.'s?
5. Will a friend please read the Tradition of the month?

It now is time to go around the room and introduce ourselves by our first name. If you are a newcomer to ACA and this is one of your first six ACA meetings, please let us know so that we may welcome you. I'll start. Again, my name is _____.

I'm going to begin passing around the Service Sign-Up Calendar. If you've been involved with ACA for at least 3 months, please consider signing up for the GREETER or CLOSER service positions at future meetings.

Keep coming back. This program is not easy, but if you can handle what comes up six meetings in a row, you will start to come out of denial. This will give you freedom from the past. Both you and your life will change. By attending six meetings in a row at the beginning and regularly attending thereafter, we come to know our true selves, and learn to behave responsibly. We do this by identifying with our common characteristics and the "ACA Solution." We choose to become our own loving parent. We come out of denial and share the pain of childhood memories. We experience love and acceptance from members of our ACA groups. We grow in awareness that experiences from the past form a pattern. We learn that pattern can change. So please keep coming back. Listen, learn, and most of all, share your feelings.

Appendix A
SAMPLE MEETING FORMAT [continued]

During our meetings, we practice self-discipline by sharing the opportunity to speak and honoring others by listening. We ask that everyone abide by the following suggestions:

- We indicate we have finished speaking with a closing statement such as "I'm finished," "I'm done," "Thank you for letting me share," etc.
- We do not interrupt someone speaking until they indicate they have finished.
- We use the words "I, me, and my" to share from our own personal experience.
- We do not "cross talk," meaning we do not refer to or comment directly on anyone else's sharing. We share our experiences only. We simply listen and do not offer advice.
- We are courteous, allowing everyone time to share. Keep shares between 3–5 minutes.
- We remember that anything heard at a meeting stays at the meeting. It is not for gossip or public disclosure. Please respect the privacy of those who share today.
- Everyone at this meeting is responsible for adhering to these safety suggestions. It is my responsibility as Chairperson to remind participants of the guidelines if necessary.

We will now move into tonight's topic which is _____. After the topic introduction is read, I'll start things off with an opening share. I'll then open up the meeting to shares from beginners … those in ACA less than a year. About halfway through the meeting, I'll open up sharing to everyone.

[BEGIN TOPIC INTRODUCTION]

Appendix A
SAMPLE MEETING FORMAT [continued]

Meeting Closing Format
- We are approaching the end of our meeting. Before we begin closing, does anyone else have a burning desire to share?
- It is now time to pass the basket for our Seventh Tradition, which states that "Every ACA group ought to be self-supporting, declining outside contributions." A suggested donation of $2.00 will ensure we will meet our financial commitments to use this room.
- While people are contributing, I want to emphasize that this is an ACA beginner's meeting. We encourage people to also attend other ACA non-beginner's meetings to learn about topics not covered here, to access additional service opportunities, and to expand their fellow traveler support network.
- Are there any other ACA-related announcements?
- Will a friend please hand out the chips?
- That's all the time we have. Thank you for joining us, and keep coming back. And now it's time for "The Promises." Would a friend please read The Promises?
- Keep coming back—it works! We will now close with the ACA Serenity Prayer

Appendix A
ACA MEETINGS WHERE I FEEL MOST COMFORTABLE

Appendix B
SHARING IN ACA MEETINGS, CROSS-TALK & FIXING

Sharing in Meetings

Many people arrive at ACA nervous and not knowing how to share at meetings. In the beginning, we encourage ACA members to share whatever comes up. There is no wrong way to share at an ACA meeting, as long as we are not verbally aggressive towards others or cross talking. ACA members listen with respect and hold space for one another with presence and empathy. After a while, our sharing might take on a general form of recalling our childhood experiences, and how we use reparenting, the Steps, and other ACA tools and resources to address the effects of family dysfunction. Sharing at ACA meetings allows us to emerge from emotional isolation by breaking the rules of family dysfunction: Don't talk–Don't trust–Don't feel. As we authentically share with others, we invite deeper connections with our true selves.

Cross Talk

In ACA, the term "cross talk" means interrupting, referring to, commenting on, or using the content of what another person has said during a meeting. Cross talk also refers to any type of dialog that occurs when the meeting is in progress. Members talking to one another or discussing what someone has just said is cross talk.

Many adult children come from family backgrounds where feelings and perceptions were constantly judged—negatively or positively. For example, we may have been told that our feelings were wrong or didn't matter–or that we were weak, stupid, or needy when we spoke up. Or we may have been praised in ways that taught us to "perform" and seek approval from others with what we say. Or, we may have grown up in environments where no one listened to us at all.

In ACA, each person may share their feelings and perceptions without fear of being judged negatively or interrupted, and without being praised in ways that can reinforce approval-seeking patterns. In ACA, we speak about our own experiences and feelings; we accept without comment what others say because it is true for them. We focus on our own healing at meetings rather than giving advice or trying to "fix" others.

In ACA, we strive to create safe places for participants to open up and share. As part of creating a safe meeting, we refrain from cross talk and fixing behaviors.

Interrupting

Each member in ACA should be able to share, free from interruption. When someone is sharing, all others should refrain from speaking, including side conversations with a neighbor. Gestures, noise, or movement could also be considered interruption if it is grossly distracting.

Appendix B
SHARING IN ACA MEETINGS, CROSS-TALK & FIXING [cont.]

Referring To

In ACA, we keep the focus on our lives and our feelings. We do not refer to the shares of others except as a transition into our own sharing. A very general "what's been brought up for me is ..." or the occasional "thank you for sharing" is fine. However, please do not make more detailed references to another person's share.

Commenting On

In ACA, we accept what each person shares as true for them. We go to great lengths to avoid creating the climate of shame that enforced the three primary rules of family dysfunction: Don't talk—Don't trust—Don't feel. In ACA, we simply do not comment positively or negatively about another person's share during a meeting. Unsolicited advice before, during, or after a meeting can be a form of commentary and should be avoided. We can ask permission if we want to speak with someone about their share after or outside a meeting. In like manner, we never talk about the contents of another person's share to a third party. Everything shared in an ACA meeting is considered privileged and confidential and must be treated with the utmost respect.

Fixing Others

In ACA, we do not touch, hug, or attempt to comfort others when they become emotional during an ACA meeting. If someone begins to cry or weep during a meeting, we allow them to feel their feelings. We support them by refraining from touching them or interrupting their tears with something we might say. To touch or hug the person in this way is known as "fixing." As children, we tried to fix our parents or to control them with our behavior. In ACA, we are learning to take care of ourselves and not attempt to fix others. We support others by accepting them into our meetings and listening to them while they face their pain. We learn to hold space by listening, letting be, and trusting the process, which is often the greatest support of all.

Appendix C
12 STEP WORKGROUPS

Introduction to ACA Workgroups

In ACA, we embrace various approaches to doing deeper recovery work with others in the program. Whether our focus is the 12 Steps, reparenting work in the Loving Parent Guidebook, or exploring and healing our adaptive childhood traits in the Laundry Lists Workbook, ACA recognizes that different approaches work well for different people at different times. Historically, in most 12 Step programs, people do concentrated recovery work one-on-one (traditionally using a sponsor/sponsee model). In ACA, adult children have explored alternative approaches to doing intensive recovery work, including being part of small, private workgroups, both in-person and online.

Doing one-on-one work can be challenging for some adult children. Growing up in our dysfunctional home environments, we learned not to talk or feel ... and we learned not to trust. In the absence of trust, many adult children developed a fear of authority in childhood (Traits 1 & 3), a desire to seek approval from those in authority (Trait 2), or reflexive reactions to fight against authority (Other Traits). Some of us tried to protect ourselves by using the power of authority and control against others (Other Traits). Therefore, some adult children can struggle with asking for, receiving, and offering support through one-on-one recovery relationships. ACA workgroups can sometimes help mitigate these dynamics.

However, workgroups can present challenges, too. Laundry Lists Traits behaviors can still arise, and members can trigger one another. While recovery requires us to stretch to try new things and work with discomfort, we need a basic sense of safety to recover. We might realize that a particular group isn't a match or that group work isn't a good fit for us at the time. It's OK to leave groups that don't work for us and find ones that do. Finding a workgroup that fits is a process and can take time.

The workgroup model can be a particularly powerful healing format for adult children. Our original wounding occurred within a dysfunctional family, so it makes sense that we might find profound healing in a small workgroup with members of our ACA family. Communal attunement and consistent connection from a group of trusted others can be transformative in our recovery process. ACA workgroups can provide what the Big Red Book calls "indirect sponsorship," and gradually, we might come to trust and rely on the group conscience for support and guidance. In time, members of our workgroup can form the foundation for our recovery support network ... each a vital source of individual experience, strength, and hope.

Appendix C
12 STEP WORKGROUPS [continued]

Creating / Joining ACA Workgroups

Duration: The ACA workgroup model usually involves working through an entire workbook as a group (12 Steps, Loving Parent Guidebook, Laundry Lists Traits, A New Hope, etc.). This format allows each participant to address all written text, questions, and exercises contained within. Completing a workbook can take anywhere from several months to over a year, depending on the pace. Most groups meet weekly for between one and two hours. Discussing time commitments up-front can help clarify individual needs and intentions as the workgroup is forming. These issues may need to be re-addressed as the group progresses and finds its own pace.

Group Size: Workgroup sizes usually range from between four and twelve members. Participants determine together what size group will work best. Newly forming workgroups sometimes stay open for the first few weeks, allowing new members to join. At some mutually agreed-upon point, the workgroup "closes" to new members. It is not uncommon for some participants to discontinue attending the group for various reasons, decreasing the workgroup size over time.

Location: The group must identify a safe and consistent place to meet each week. Usually, in-person workgroups meet in the home of one of the participants. Alternative locations might include non-profit centers with private meeting spaces such as hospitals, places of worship, or 12 Step clubhouses. Online workgroups will need to identify a platform (such as Zoom, Facebook, Teams, Hangouts, Skype, etc.) and who will have access to and be responsible for starting and hosting meetings. It's important to develop contingencies if the person hosting the meeting (either in-person or online) can't make it or doesn't show.

Format: The process of going through any of the ACA workbooks will involve reading, writing, sharing, and witnessing. Groups may choose to *read* through the large text sections in the workbook together, taking turns and pausing for discussion. Or workgroups may agree to read sections ahead of time on their own and come prepared to discuss. *Writing* can involve answering questions or doing other types of written exercises. It is suggested that participants do the written sections ahead of time on their own. However, most workgroups don't require anyone to do this type of "homework." Most groups read sequentially through all questions together, allowing each participant to *share* their responses or pass. Finally, *witnessing* is one of the most important parts of the ACA workgroup healing process. Participants quietly and attentively listen as each member courageously breaks the old rules of family dysfunction: Don't talk—Don't trust—Don't feel.

Safety Guidelines: New workgroups are encouraged to create safety agreements. Some groups write out guidelines; others do not. Topics may include time/duration

Appendix C
12 STEP WORKGROUPS [continued]

commitments to the group, attendance & missing meetings, phone/electronics use, alcohol/drug/food use, crosstalk & fixing, sharing time limits, confidentiality, etc. Safety guidelines can be revisited and adjusted if group member needs change.

Experience & "Expertise": Having one or more people in a workgroup with previous ACA workgroup experience can be beneficial. However, including a "veteran" participant isn't always possible, nor is having a more experienced member required (nor sometimes even desired). Anyone in ACA can start a workgroup. There are no workgroup "experts" or "authorities" in ACA.

Questions, Conflict & Authority: ACA workgroups can help ease authority-related Laundry Lists Traits effects for some people. Still, authority issues in group work, just like in one-on-one work, can and do surface. Some adult children seek to make others an authority who will "give them all the answers." Others reflexively react with hostility if they feel someone is telling them what to do. Some adult children protect themselves by trying to assert control in authoritative ways. When questions and conflicts arise, participants are encouraged to address them together openly, honestly, and directly. Resolving conflict in the spirit of the workgroup's safety guidelines, adhering to ACA Traditions, and with as much gentleness, patience, love, and respect as possible can be healing and empowering. To support group safety, participants are encouraged to ask ACA fellow travelers outside the workgroup for their experience, strength, and hope in ways that do not breach the workgroup's confidentiality. Addressing disagreement and conflict can be challenging for adult children. Yet, it can also be an opportunity to deepen one's growth and recovery process.

For 12 Step Work—Other Laundry List Use: The Other Laundry List Traits were more formally developed after the yellow 12 Step workbook was created. Some workgroups choose to include this information in their 12 Step work. If a group wishes, the Other Laundry List Traits can be referenced whenever the standard Laundry List Traits are presented throughout the ACA 12 Step yellow workbook.

For 12 Step Work—Tony A's 12 Steps Use: Tony A's version of the 12 Steps is not in the yellow workbook due to copyright issues. Still, some workgroups choose to include this information in their 12 Step work. A group can decide to introduce and reference Tony A's version of the 12 Steps when the standard ACA 12 Steps are referenced in the ACA 12 Step yellow workbook, so long as the group does not violate copyright laws.

Additional Workgroup Resources for the Loving Parent Guidebook: Available at https://adultchildren.org/literature/loving-parent-guidebook/

Appendix C
12 STEP WORKGROUPS [continued]

ACA WORKGROUP SAMPLE SAFETY GUIDELINES

The following are some sample safety suggestions. Each workgroup determines for itself what guidelines to put in place to support safety. Guidelines can be revisited and modified over time.

- Please arrive on time to be considerate of other group members. Members agree to notify at least one other participant ahead of time if they will not be attending a workgroup meeting. Regular attendance is recommended.*
- Please do not attend workgroup meetings if under the influence of illicit substances or alcohol.
- Please silence (preferably turn off) and put away electronic devices upon arrival to reduce possibilities for distraction and interruption.
- Please be mindful of equitable sharing times, allowing all participants equal opportunities to share. A three-minute-per-share limit (with some exceptions now and then) is recommended.**
- Please respect participants' freedom to pass and share at the level that feels comfortable to them.
- Please do not interrupt other members when they are sharing.
- Please use the words "I, me, and my" to share from your personal experience.
- Please do not "cross talk," which for this group means not referring to, commenting directly on, or judging/criticizing anyone else's sharing. We simply listen and do not offer advice. Attentively listening to others as they face their pain can often be the greatest support of all.
- Please respect the privacy of those who share. What is communicated at our workgroup meeting stays at this meeting.

---

* Long absences may threaten workgroup safety. Therefore, some groups choose to set specific boundaries around attendance, such as limits on consecutive absences, or the total number of workgroup meetings missed.
** Some groups time participant shares for various lengths of time. Others do not.

Appenix D
ABOUT THIS WORKBOOK

Handbook Principles

- Family Dysfunction: This handbook strives to increase inclusivity by clearly summarizing the various expressions of family dysfunction beyond alcoholism so more people can benefit from ACA as a program of recovery.

- Trauma Recovery vs. Addictions Recovery: Whereas most Twelve Step programs are understood to be addiction recovery programs, this Handbook understands ACA to be primarily a trauma recovery program. This distinction presents unique 12 Step program "translation" considerations, which this Handbook attempts to address.

- Laundry Lists Traits: Both the Laundry List Traits and the Other/Opposite Laundry Lists Traits are presented up-front as part of this Handbook. Both lists present a wide range of childhood trauma expressions that adult children can experience, and heal through ACA recovery work.

- 12 Steps: While the ACA 12 Steps are presented in this Handbook as foundational in ACA recovery, Tony A.'s 12 Steps are also mentioned. Many in ACA identify strongly with Tony's version of the Steps and include it in their recovery work. Although copyright law prohibits copying or distributing Tony A's steps, we are not prohibited from creating new sets of steps that are more gentle and loving. The Literature Committee of the World Service Organization will be presenting additional sets of steps to ACA members for their use by group conscience. Additionally, this Handbook embraces the notion that "ACA members work the Steps in order, avoiding looking ahead and perhaps becoming overwhelmed" (BRB). Therefore, this Handbook for beginners provides only a general overview of the 12 Steps and an introduction to Step 1. However, the concepts and principles of all the Steps are indirectly presented. For example: "Inner Loving Parent," "Inner Child," and "Spirituality" (Steps 2 and 3), "Childhood Trauma" (Step 4), "Grief" (Step 5), etc.

- Spiritual Inclusivity: This Handbook takes to heart that ACA is a spiritual and not a religious program—atheists, agnostics, and believers are all welcome and valued:

    – Belief in a personified or anthropomorphized deity is not required for ACA healing—spiritually or otherwise. However, exploring resources beyond one's current awareness and seeking out powers greater than oneself is essential.

    – Some spiritual teachers say that a finger pointing at the moon is not itself the moon. The term "higher power(s)" and similar terms and phrases such as "resources beyond one's current awareness" and "powers greater than oneself"

Appenix D
ABOUT THIS WORKBOOK [continued]

are used to point towards something. These terms used in this way are not proper nouns. Therefore, they are not capitalized in this Handbook, except when referencing other ACA literature where these terms have been capitalized.

- The term "higher power(s)" in this Handbook is used without reference to gender.
- The term "higher power(s)" in this Handbook makes beginning attempts not to reference singular or plural designation for higher power(s).
- The term "God" is not used unless when referencing existing ACA literature or in first-person accounts.

- <u>Fellow Traveler Model:</u> This Handbook takes to heart the 1989 ACA Sponsorship Committee's caution about the traditional AA sponsorship model when it states that it does not "adequately address the tendencies of the ACA personality, namely our over-reliance on others for direction and approval and our tendency to try to manage someone else's life." Without a modification to that model, it was feared that a sponsor may dominate a sponsee who may be willing to give up personal freedom and choice. Therefore, that Committee recommended the "fellow traveler" or co-sponsor approach for healthy peer-to-peer recovery relationships in ACA. More recent ACA literature recommends that members choose the form of support that works for them, whether it is a sponsor, a fellow traveler, a co-sponsor, a recovery partner, or other term. In all forms of support, one person speaks honestly and openly with trust and the other person listens intently and speaks gently and lovingly, using the voice of the inner loving parent.

- <u>Service:</u> This Handbook frames service work in ACA as an extension of service to self (ACA Identity Report #3, section "Re-Emergence of the United Self"). Therefore, this Handbook examines ACA service work within the context of the Laundry Lists Traits and presents healthy service to others as being in alignment with the ACA Solution of reparenting.

Appendix E
ACA FOUNDATIONAL MATERIALS

Laundry Lists Traits

                                        Ever Applied? ✓   Applies today? ✓

1. We became isolated and afraid of people and authority figures.
2. We became approval seekers and lost our identity in the process.
3. We are frightened by angry people and any personal criticism.
4. We either become alcoholics, marry them or both, or find another compulsive personality such as a workaholic to fulfill our sick abandonment needs.
5. We live life from the viewpoint of victims, and we are attracted by that weakness in our love and friendship relationships.
6. We have an overdeveloped sense of responsibility and it is easier for us to be concerned with others rather than ourselves; this enables us not to look too closely at our own faults, etc.
7. We get guilt feelings when we stand up for ourselves instead of giving in to others.
8. We became addicted to excitement (fear / chaos / drama).
9. We confuse love and pity and tend to "love" people we can "pity" and "rescue."
10. We have "stuffed" our feelings from our traumatic childhoods and have lost the ability to feel or express our feelings because it hurts so much (Denial).
11. We judge ourselves harshly and have a very low sense of self-esteem.
12. We are dependent personalities who are terrified of abandonment and will do anything to hold on to a relationship in order not to experience painful abandonment feelings, which we received from living with sick people who were never there emotionally for us.
13. Alcoholism is a family disease; and we became para-alcoholics and took on the characteristics of that disease even though we did not pick up the drink.
14. Para-alcoholics are reactors rather than actors.

Appendix E
ACA FOUNDATIONAL MATERIALS

Other / Opposite Laundry Lists Traits

	Ever Applied? ✓	Applies today? ✓

1. To cover our fear of people and our dread of isolation we tragically become the very authority figures who frighten others and cause them to withdraw. _____ _____
2. To avoid becoming enmeshed and entangled with other people and losing ourselves in the process, we become rigidly self-sufficient. We disdain the approval of others. _____ _____
3. We frighten people with our anger and threat of belittling criticism.
4. We dominate others and abandon them before they can abandon us or we avoid relationships with dependent people altogether. To avoid being hurt, we isolate and dissociate and thereby abandon ourselves. _____ _____
5. We live life from the standpoint of a victimizer, and are attracted to people we can manipulate and control in our important relationships. _____ _____
6. We are irresponsible and self-centered. Our inflated sense of self-worth and self-importance prevents us from seeing our deficiencies and shortcomings. _____ _____
7. We make others feel guilty when they attempt to assert themselves. _____ _____
8. We inhibit our fear by staying deadened and numb. _____ _____
9. We hate people who "play" the victim and beg to be rescued. _____ _____
10. We deny that we've been hurt and are suppressing our emotions by the dramatic expression of "pseudo" feelings. _____ _____
11. To protect ourselves from self-punishment for failing to "save" the family we project our self-hate onto others and punish them instead. _____ _____
12. We "manage" the massive amount of deprivation we feel, coming from abandonment within the home, by quickly letting go of relationships that threaten our "independence" (not too close). _____ _____
13. We refuse to admit we've been affected by family dysfunction or that there was dysfunction in the home or that we have internalized any of the family's destructive attitudes and behaviors. _____ _____
14. We act as if we are nothing like the dependent people who raised us. _____ _____

Appendix E
ACA FOUNDATIONAL MATERIALS

ACA Laundry Lists Framework

ACA co-founder Tony A. wrote the 14 Traits of an adult child of an alcoholic in 1978. From the descriptive power of the Traits, ACA was born and created. In just 260 words, **The Laundry List** describes the thinking and personality of an adult reared in a dysfunctional family. **The Other Laundry List** (also known as Opposite Laundry List) points out that as adults, we might, in turn, "act out" those Traits by becoming victimizers. In other words, adult children, by adopting their parents' behaviors, "become" their parents. **The Flip Side of the Laundry List** and **The Flip Side of the Other Laundry List** detail how, through reparenting and practising the ACA Twelve Steps, we might be freed from these effects. This Laundry Lists Framework is for ACAs who are ready to embark on *advanced work* on their survival traits, and the ACA "Laundry Lists Workbook" is designed for ACAs who have already gone through all the Steps in the ACA "Twelve Steps Workbook".

	Laundry List	Other Laundry List
TRAIT 1	**We became isolated and afraid of people and authority figures.**	To cover our fear of people and our dread of isolation we tragically become the very authority figures who frighten others and cause them to withdraw.
	Flip Side of the Laundry List	Flip Side of the Other Laundry List
	We move out of isolation and are not unrealistically afraid of other people, even authority figures.	We face and resolve our fear of people and our dread of isolation and stop intimidating others with our power and position.

	Laundry List	Other Laundry List
TRAIT 2	**We became approval seekers and lost our identity in the process.**	To avoid becoming enmeshed and entangled with other people and losing ourselves in the process, we become rigidly self-sufficient. We disdain the approval of others.
	Flip Side of the Laundry List	Flip Side of the Other Laundry List
	We do not depend on others to tell us who we are.	We realize the sanctuary we have built to protect the frightened and injured child within has become a prison and we become willing to risk moving out of isolation.

	Laundry List	Other Laundry List
TRAIT 3	**We are frightened by angry people and any personal criticism.**	We frighten people with our anger and threat of belittling criticism.
	Flip Side of the Laundry List	Flip Side of the Other Laundry List
	We are not automatically frightened by angry people and no longer regard personal criticism as a threat.	With our renewed sense of self-worth and self-esteem we realize it is no longer necessary to protect ourselves by intimidating others with contempt, ridicule and anger.

Appendix E
ACA FOUNDATIONAL MATERIALS

	Laundry List	Other Laundry List
TRAIT 4	**We either become alcoholics, marry them or both, or find another compulsive personality such as a workaholic to fulfill our sick abandonment needs.**	We dominate others and abandon them before they can abandon us or we avoid relationships with dependent people altogether. To avoid being hurt, we isolate and dissociate and thereby abandon ourselves.
	Flip Side of the Laundry List	*Flip Side of the Other Laundry List*
	We do not have a compulsive need to recreate abandonment.	We accept and comfort the isolated and hurt inner child we have abandoned and disavowed and thereby end the need to act out our fears of enmeshment and abandonment with other people.

	Laundry List	Other Laundry List
TRAIT 5	**We live life from the viewpoint of victims and we are attracted by that weakness in our love and friendship relationships.**	We live life from the standpoint of a victimizer, and are attracted to people we can manipulate and control in our important relationships.
	Flip Side of the Laundry List	*Flip Side of the Other Laundry List*
	We stop living life from the standpoint of victims and are not attracted by this trait in our important relationships.	Because we are whole and complete we no longer try to control others through manipulation and force and bind them to us with fear in order to avoid feeling isolated and alone.

	Laundry List	Other Laundry List
TRAIT 6	**We have an overdeveloped sense of responsibility and it is easier for us to be concerned with others rather than ourselves; this enables us not to look too closely at our own faults, etc.**	We are irresponsible and self-centered. Our inflated sense of self-worth and self-importance prevents us from seeing our deficiencies and shortcomings.
	Flip Side of the Laundry List	*Flip Side of the Other Laundry List*
	We do not use enabling as a way to avoid looking at our own shortcomings.	Through our in-depth inventory we discover our true identity as capable, worthwhile people. By asking to have our shortcomings removed we are freed from the burden of inferiority and grandiosity.

	Laundry List	Other Laundry List
TRAIT 7	**We get guilt feelings when we stand up for ourselves instead of giving in to others.**	We make others feel guilty when they attempt to assert themselves.
	Flip Side of the Laundry List	*Flip Side of the Other Laundry List*
	We do not feel guilty when we stand up for ourselves.	We support and encourage others in their efforts to be assertive.

Appendix E
ACA FOUNDATIONAL MATERIALS

	Laundry List	Other Laundry List
TRAIT 8	We became addicted to excitement.	We inhibit our fear by staying deadened and numb.
	Flip Side of the Laundry List	*Flip Side of the Other Laundry List*
	We avoid emotional intoxication and choose workable relationships instead of constant upset.	We uncover, acknowledge and express our childhood fears and withdraw from emotional intoxication.

	Laundry List	Other Laundry List
TRAIT 9	We confuse love and pity and tend to "love" people we can "pity" and "rescue."	We hate people who "play" the victim and beg to be rescued.
	Flip Side of the Laundry List	*Flip Side of the Other Laundry List*
	We are able to distinguish love from pity, and do not think "rescuing" people we "pity" is an act of love.	We have compassion for anyone who is trapped in the "drama triangle" and is desperately searching for a way out of insanity.

	Laundry List	Other Laundry List
TRAIT 10	We have "stuffed" our feelings from our traumatic childhoods and have lost the ability to feel or express our feelings because it hurts so much (denial).	We deny that we've been hurt and are suppressing our emotions by the dramatic expression of "pseudo" feelings.
	Flip Side of the Laundry List	*Flip Side of the Other Laundry List*
	We come out of denial about our traumatic childhoods and regain the ability to feel and express our emotions.	We accept we were traumatized in childhood and lost the ability to feel. Using the 12 Steps as a program of recovery we regain the ability to feel and remember and become whole human beings who are happy, joyous and free.

	Laundry List	Other Laundry List
TRAIT 11	We judge ourselves harshly and have a very low sense of self-esteem.	To protect ourselves from self-punishment for failing to "save" the family we project our self-hate onto others and punish them instead.
	Flip Side of the Laundry List	*Flip Side of the Other Laundry List*
	We stop judging and condemning ourselves and discover a sense of self-worth.	In accepting we were powerless as children to "save" our family we are able to release our self-hate and to stop punishing ourselves and others for not being enough.

Appendix E
ACA FOUNDATIONAL MATERIALS

	Laundry List	Other Laundry List
TRAIT 12	**We are dependent personalities who are terrified of abandonment and will do anything to hold on to a relationship in order not to experience painful abandonment feelings, which we received from living with sick people who were never there emotionally for us.**	We "manage" the massive amount of deprivation we feel, coming from abandonment within the home, by quickly letting go of relationships that threaten our "independence" (not too close).
	Flip Side of the Laundry List	*Flip Side of the Other Laundry List*
	We grow in independence and are no longer terrified of abandonment. We have interdependent relationships with healthy people, not dependent relationships with people who are emotionally unavailable.	By accepting and reuniting with the inner child we are no longer threatened by intimacy, by the fear of being engulfed or made invisible.

	Laundry List	Other Laundry List
TRAIT 13	**Alcoholism is a family disease; and we became para-alcoholics and took on the characteristics of that disease even though we did not pick up the drink.**	We refuse to admit we've been affected by family dysfunction or that there was dysfunction in the home or that we have internalized any of the family's destructive attitudes and behaviors.
	Flip Side of the Laundry List	*Flip Side of the Other Laundry List*
	The characteristics of alcoholism and para-alcoholism we have internalized are identified, acknowledged, and removed.	By acknowledging the reality of family dysfunction we no longer have to act as if nothing were wrong or keep denying that we are still unconsciously reacting to childhood harm and injury.

	Laundry List	Other Laundry List
TRAIT 14	**Para-alcoholics are reactors rather than actors.**	We act as if we are nothing like the dependent people who raised us.
	Flip Side of the Laundry List	*Flip Side of the Other Laundry List*
	We are actors, not reactors.	We stop denying and do something about our post-traumatic dependency on substances, people, places and things to distort and avoid reality.

Appendix E
ACA FOUNDATIONAL MATERIALS

ACA Problem

Many of us found that we had several characteristics in common as a result of being brought up in an alcoholic or dysfunctional household. We had come to feel isolated and uneasy with other people, especially authority figures. To protect ourselves, we became people-pleasers, even though we lost our own identities in the process. All the same we would mistake any personal criticism as a threat. We either became alcoholics (or practiced other addictive behavior) ourselves, or married them, or both. Failing that, we found other compulsive personalities, such as a workaholic, to fulfill our sick need for abandonment.

We lived life from the standpoint of victims. Having an overdeveloped sense of responsibility, we preferred to be concerned with others rather than ourselves. We got guilt feelings when we stood up for ourselves rather than giving in to others. Thus, we became reactors, rather than actors, letting others take the initiative. We were dependent personalities, terrified of abandonment, willing to do almost anything to hold on to a relationship in order not to be abandoned emotionally. Yet we kept choosing insecure relationships because they matched our childhood relationship with alcoholic or dysfunctional parents. These symptoms of the family disease of alcoholism or other dysfunction made us "co-victims," those who take on the characteristics of the disease without necessarily ever taking a drink. We learned to keep our feelings down as children and kept them buried as adults. As a result of this conditioning, we confused love with pity, tending to love those we could rescue. Even more self-defeating, we became addicted to excitement in all our affairs, preferring constant upset to workable relationships.

This is a description, not an indictment.

Appendix E
ACA FOUNDATIONAL MATERIALS

ACA Solution

"The ACA Solution is to become your own loving parent."

As ACA becomes a safe place for you, you will find freedom to express all the hurts and fears you have kept inside and to free yourself from the shame and blame that are carryovers from the past. You will become an adult who is imprisoned no longer by childhood reactions. You will recover the child within you, learning to accept and love yourself.

The healing begins when we risk moving out of isolation. Feelings and buried memories will return. By gradually releasing the burden of unexpressed grief, we slowly move out of the past. We learn to re-parent ourselves with gentleness, humor, love and respect.

This process allows us to see our biological parents as the instruments of our existence. Our actual parent is a higher power whom some of us choose to call God. Although we had alcoholic or dysfunctional parents, our higher power gave us the Twelve Steps of Recovery.

This is the action and work that heals us: we use the Steps; we use the meetings; we use the telephone. We share our experience, strength, and hope with each other. We learn to restructure our sick thinking one day at a time. When we release our parents from responsibility for our actions today, we become free to make healthful decisions as actors, not reactors. We progress from hurting, to healing, to helping. We awaken to a sense of wholeness we never knew was possible.

By attending these meetings on a regular basis, you will come to see parental alcoholism or family dysfunction for what it is: a disease that infected you as a child and continues to affect you as an adult. You will learn to keep the focus on yourself in the here and now. You will take responsibility for your own life and supply your own parenting.

You will not do this alone. Look around you and you will see others who know how you feel. We will love and encourage you no matter what. We ask you to accept us just as we accept you.

This is a spiritual program based on action coming from love. We are sure that as the love grows inside you, you will see beautiful changes in all your relationships, especially with your higher power, yourself, and your parents.

Appendix E
ACA FOUNDATIONAL MATERIALS

ACA Twelve Steps

1. We admitted we were powerless over the effects of alcoholism or other family dysfunction, that our lives had become unmanageable.
2. Came to believe that a power greater than ourselves could restore us to sanity.
3. Made a decision to turn our will and our lives over to the care of God as we understand God.
4. Made a searching and fearless moral inventory of ourselves.
5. Admitted to God, to ourselves, and to another human being the exact nature of our wrongs.
6. Were entirely ready to have God remove all these defects of character.
7. Humbly asked God to remove our shortcomings.
8. Made a list of all persons we had harmed and became willing to make amends to them all.
9. Made direct amends to such people wherever possible, except when to do so would injure them or others.
10. Continued to take personal inventory and, when we were wrong, promptly admitted it.
11. Sought through prayer and meditation to improve our conscious contact with God, as we understand God, praying only for knowledge of God's will for us and the power to carry that out.
12. Having had a spiritual awakening as a result of these steps, we tried to carry this message to others who still suffer, and to practice these principles in all our affairs.

Appendix E
ACA FOUNDATIONAL MATERIALS

Twelve Steps—Tony A.'s version

Note: Tony A's steps are copyright protected and, therefore, cannot be published in this book without permission. That permission was requested but denied when it was sought by the Adult Children of Alcoholics & Dysfunctional Families World Service Organization (WSO).

Appendix E
ACA FOUNDATIONAL MATERIALS

ACA Twelve Traditions

1. Our common welfare should come first; personal recovery depends on ACA unity.
2. For our group purpose there is but one ultimate authority—a loving God as expressed in our group conscience. Our leaders are but trusted servants, they do not govern.
3. The only requirement for membership in ACA is a desire to recover from the effects of growing up in an alcoholic or otherwise dysfunctional family.
4. Each group is autonomous except in matters affecting other groups or ACA as a whole. We cooperate with all other Twelve-Step programs.
5. Each group has but one primary purpose—to carry its message to the adult child who still suffers.
6. An ACA group ought never endorse, finance or lend the ACA name to any related facility or outside enterprise, lest problems of money, property and prestige divert us from our primary purpose.
7. Every ACA group ought to be fully self-supporting, declining outside contributions.
8. Adult Children of Alcoholics should remain forever non-professional, but our service centers may employ special workers.
9. ACA, as such, ought never be organized, but we may create service boards or committees directly responsible to those they serve.
10. Adult Children of Alcoholics has no opinion on outside issues; hence the ACA name ought never be drawn into public controversy.
11. Our public relations policy is based on attraction rather than promotion; we maintain personal anonymity at the level of press, radio, TV, films, and other public media.
12. Anonymity is the spiritual foundation of all our Traditions, ever reminding us to place principles before personalities.

Appendix E
ACA FOUNDATIONAL MATERIALS

ACA Promises

1. We will discover our real identities by loving and accepting ourselves.
2. Our self-esteem will increase as we give ourselves approval on a daily basis.
3. Fear of authority figures and the need to "people-please" will leave us.
4. Our ability to share intimacy will grow inside us.
5. As we face our abandonment issues, we will be attracted by strengths and become more tolerant of weaknesses.
6. We will enjoy feeling stable, peaceful, and financially secure.
7. We will learn how to play and have fun in our lives.
8. We will choose to love people who can love and be responsible for themselves.
9. Healthy boundaries and limits will become easier for us to set.
10. Fears of failure and success will leave us, as we intuitively make healthier choices.
11. With help from our ACA support group, we will slowly release our dysfunctional behaviors.
12. Gradually, with our higher power's help, we will learn to expect the best and get it.

Appendix E
NOTES

Appendix E
NOTES

Appendix E
NOTES

Appendix E
NOTES